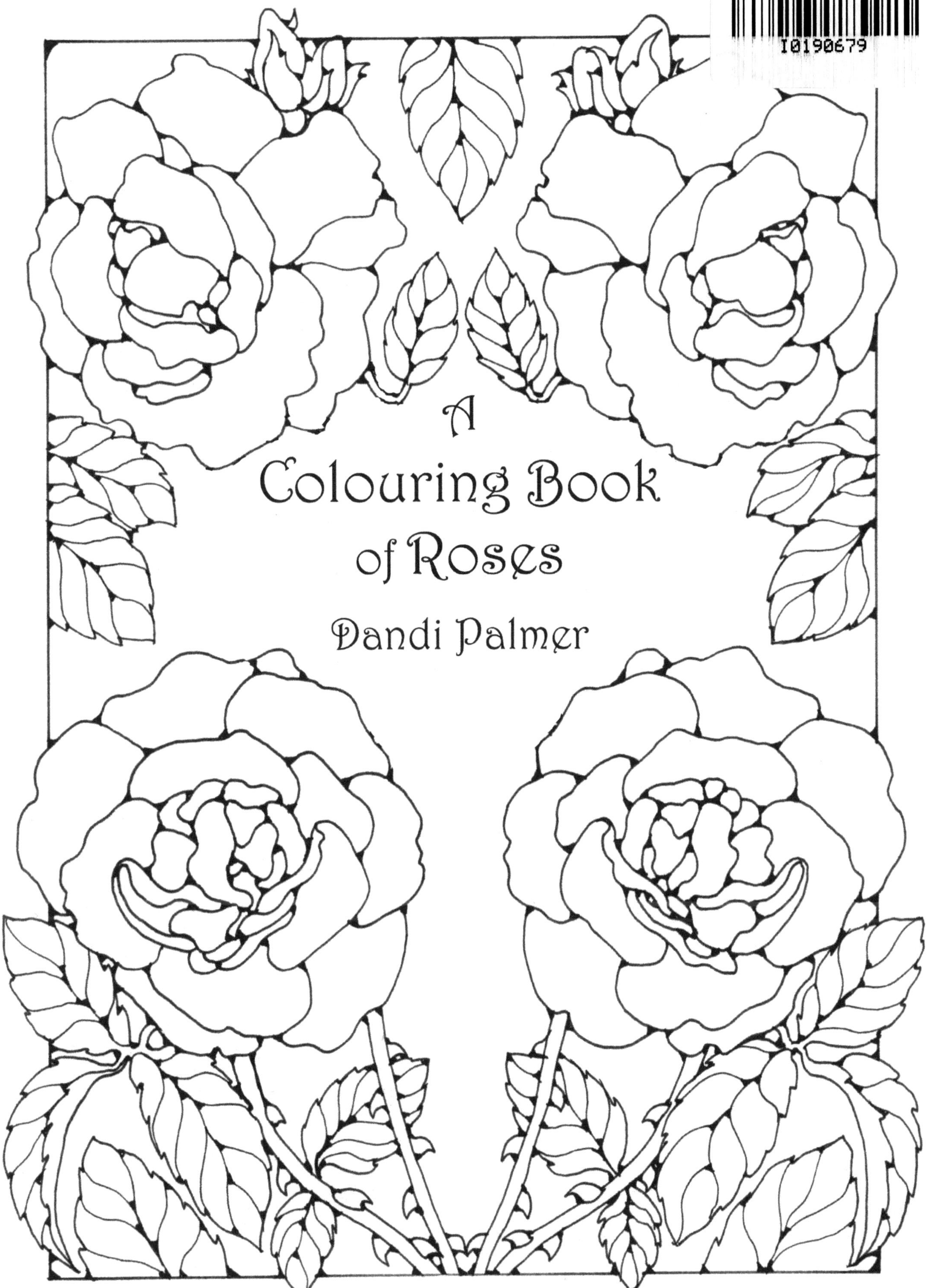

A Colouring Book of Roses

Dandi Palmer

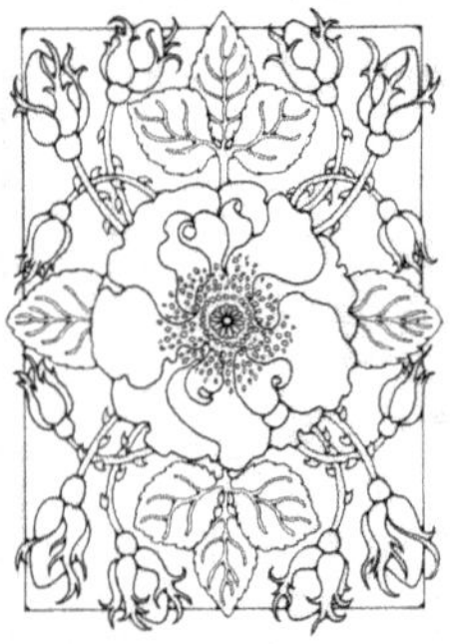
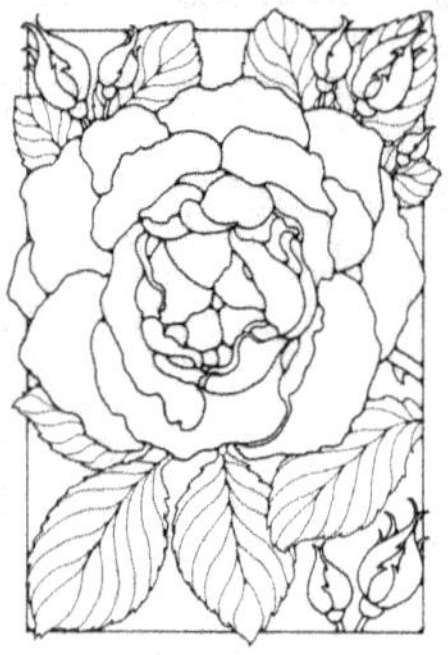
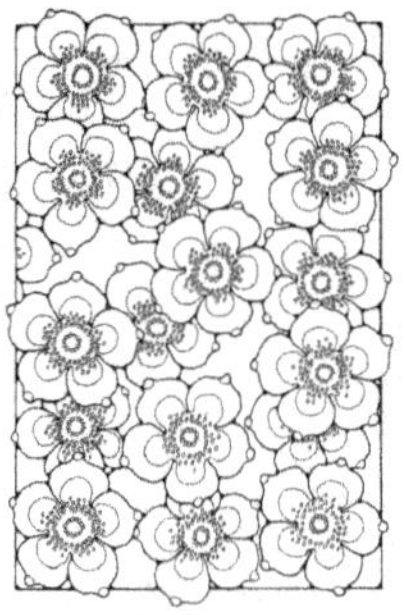
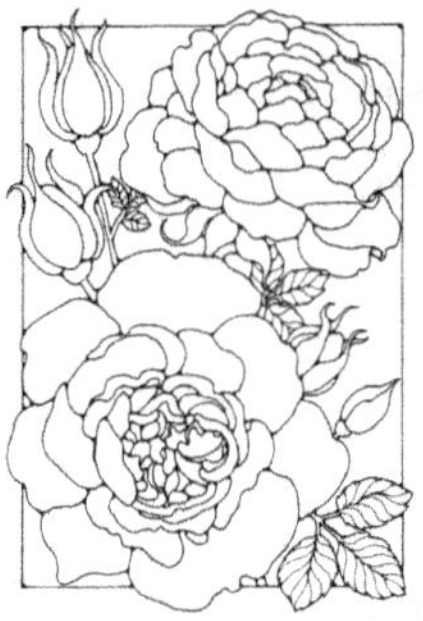
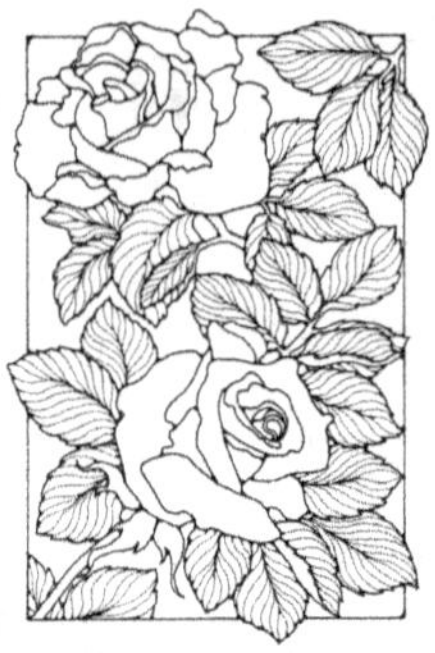
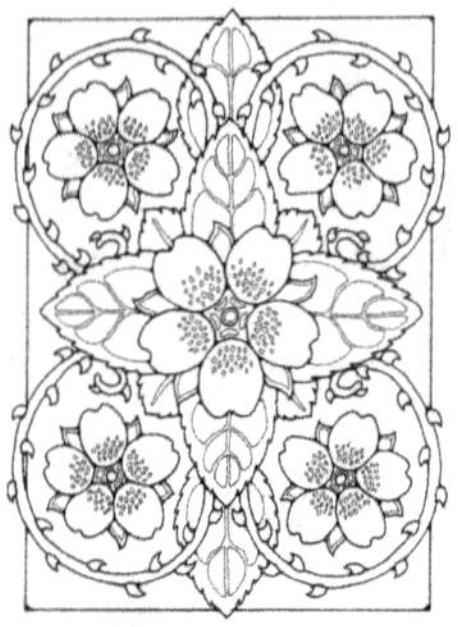
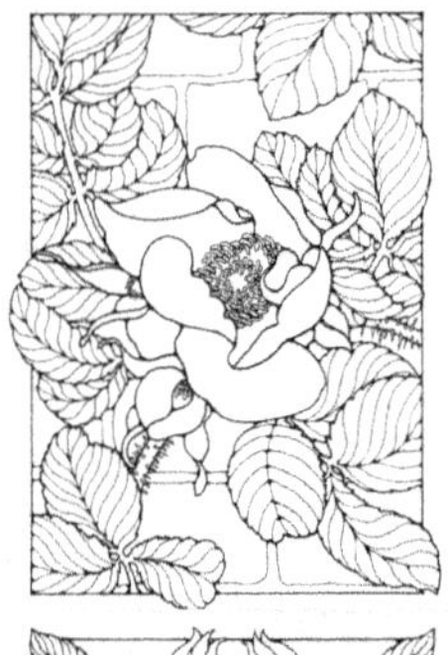
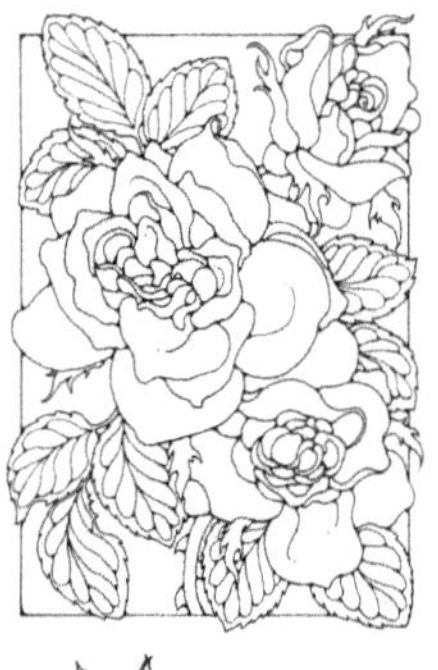
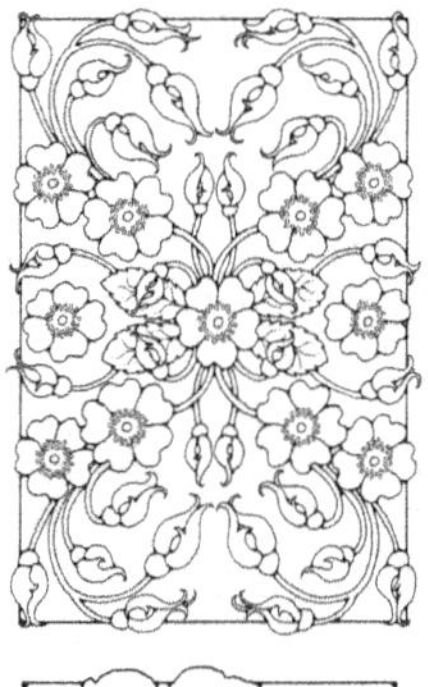
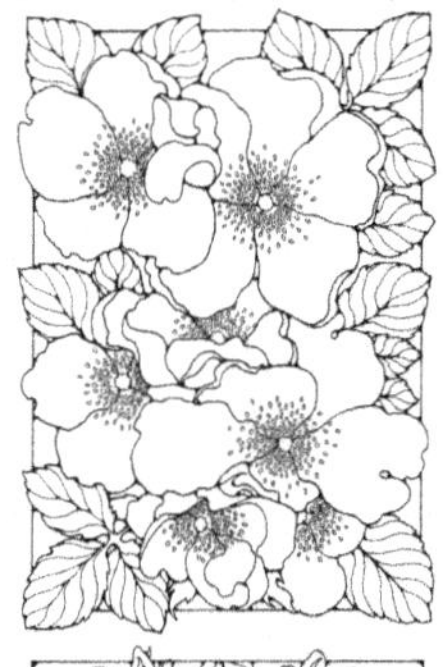
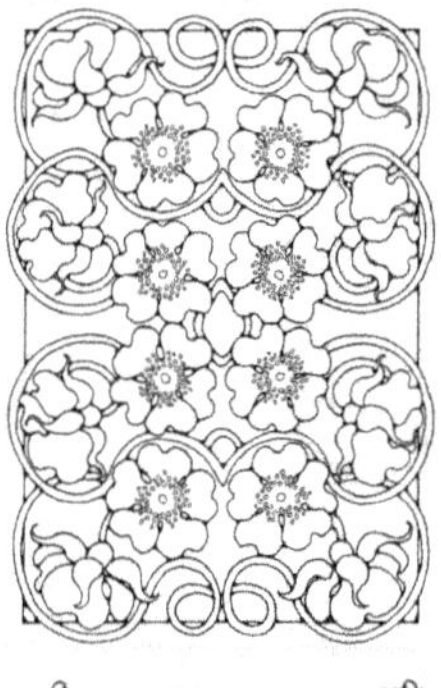
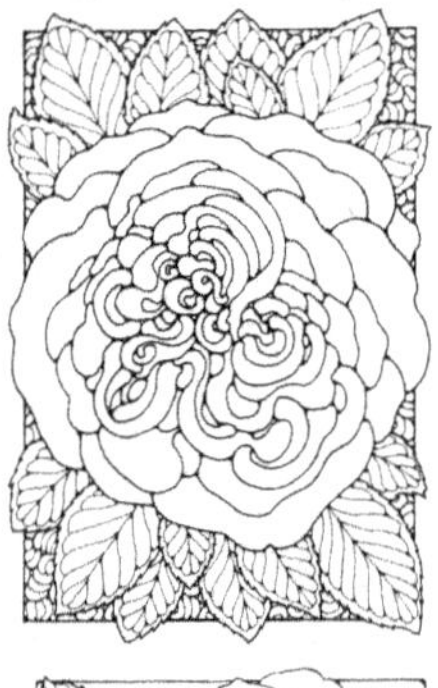
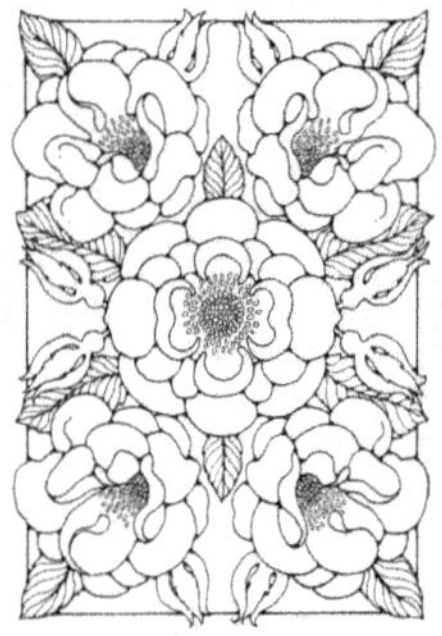
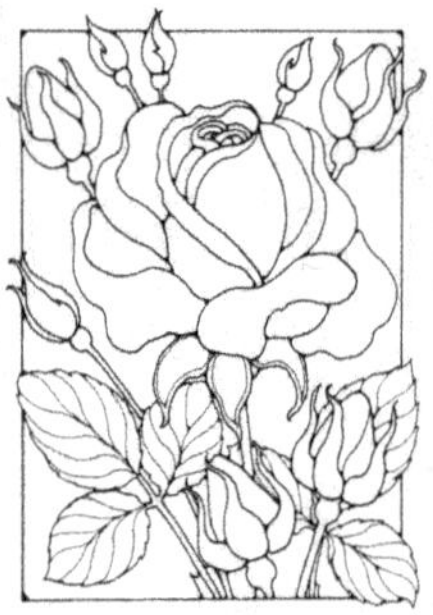
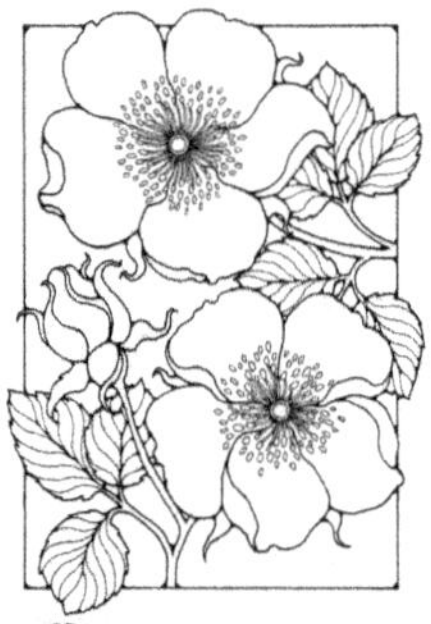
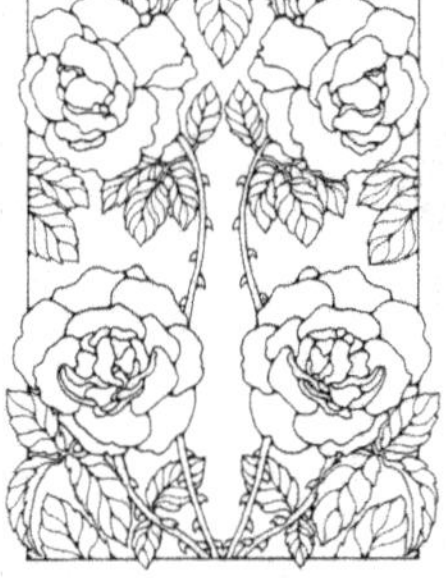
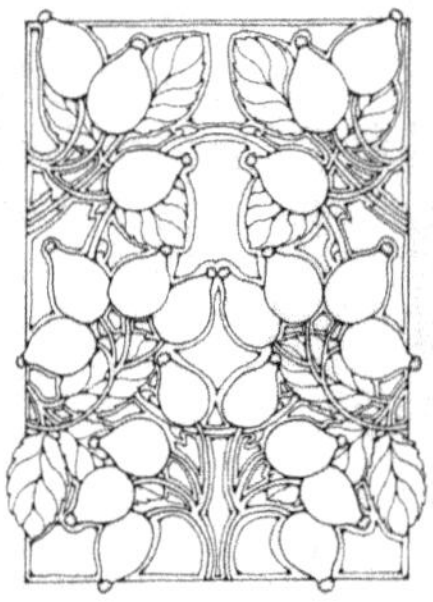
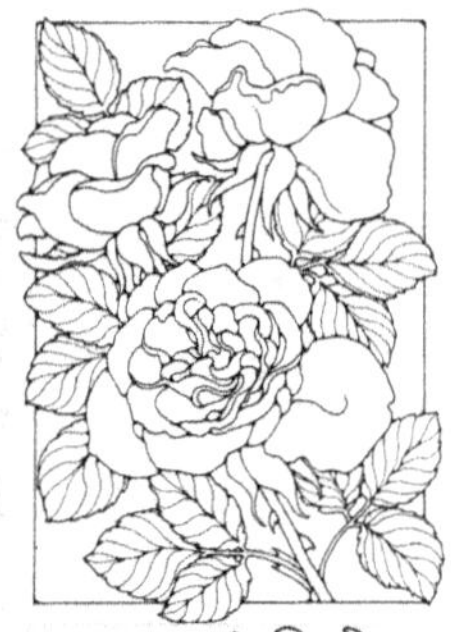
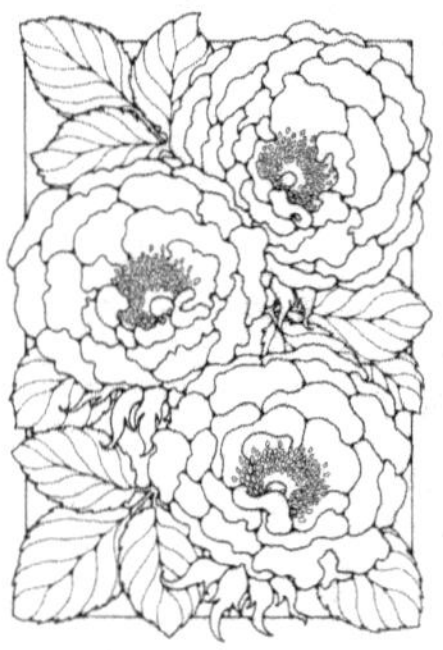
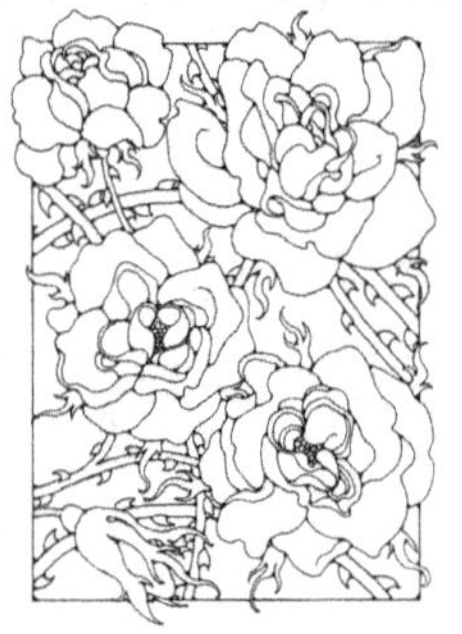
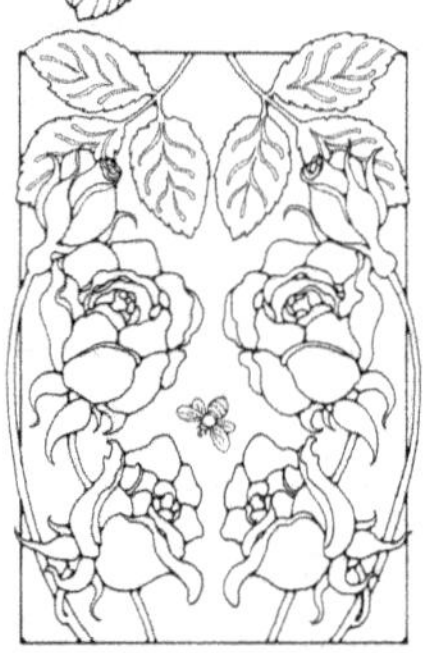
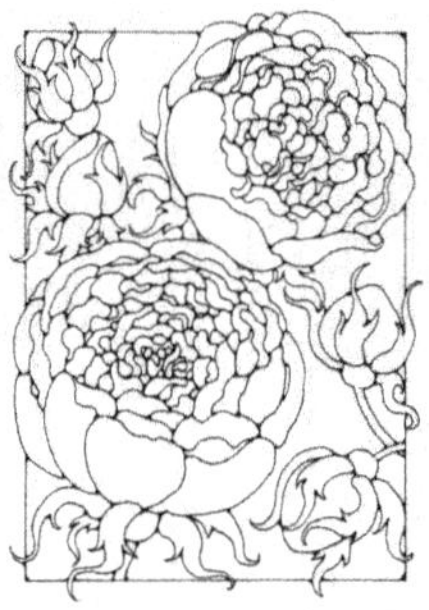
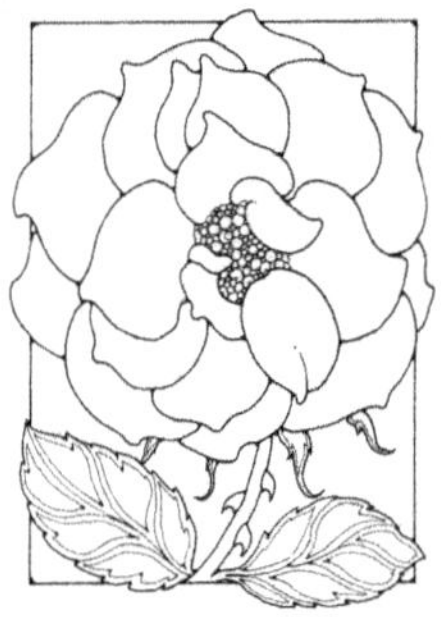
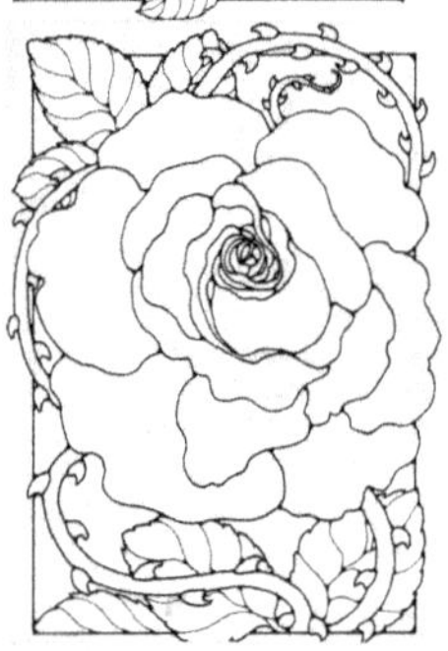
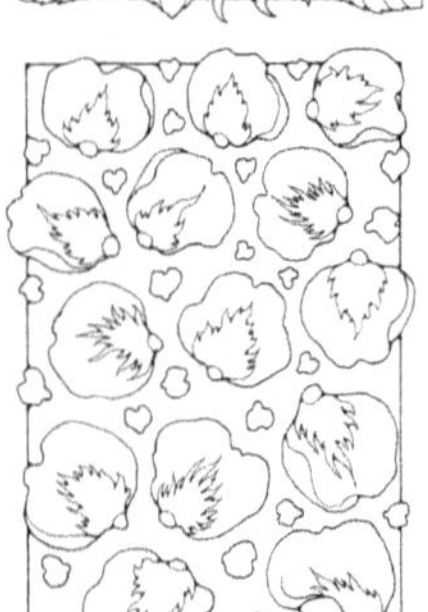
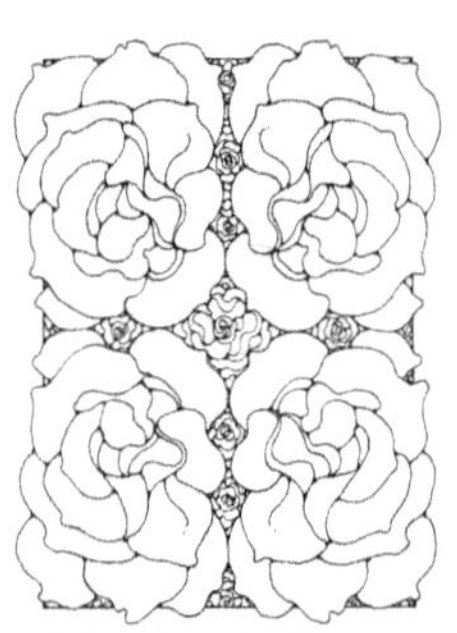
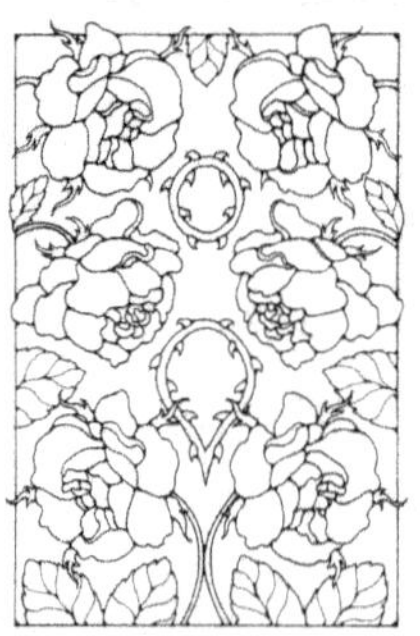
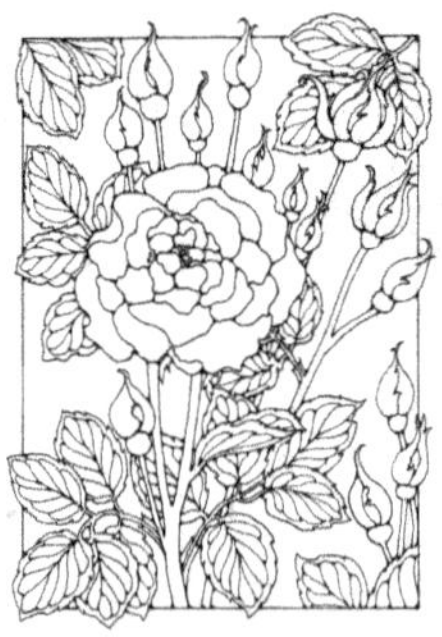
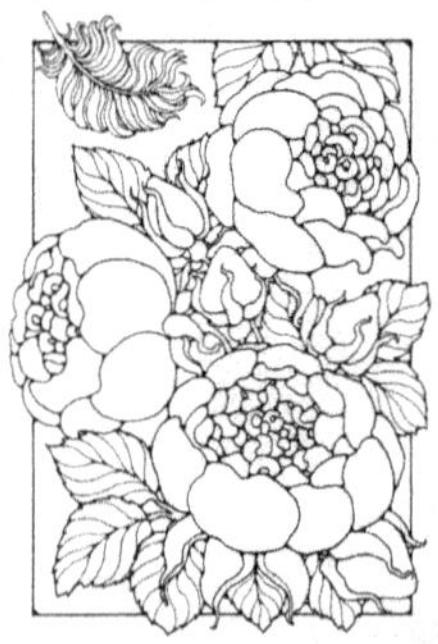
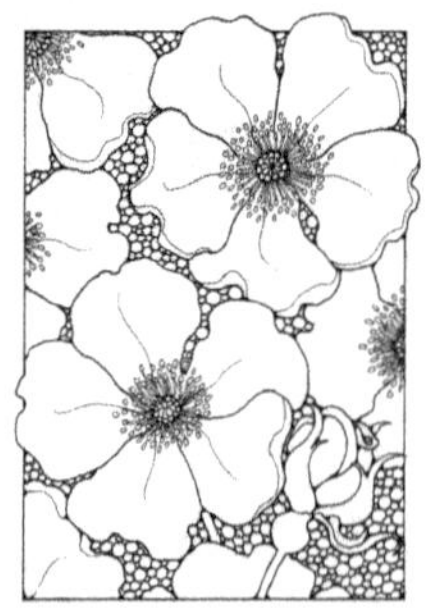
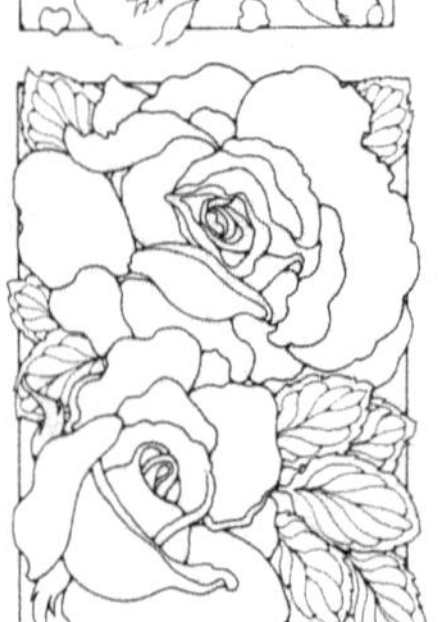
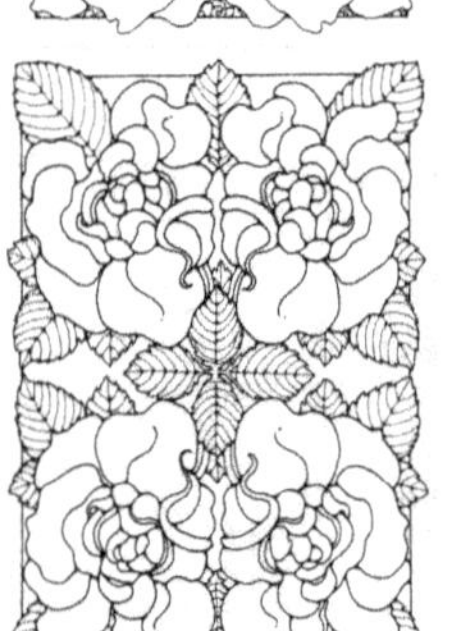
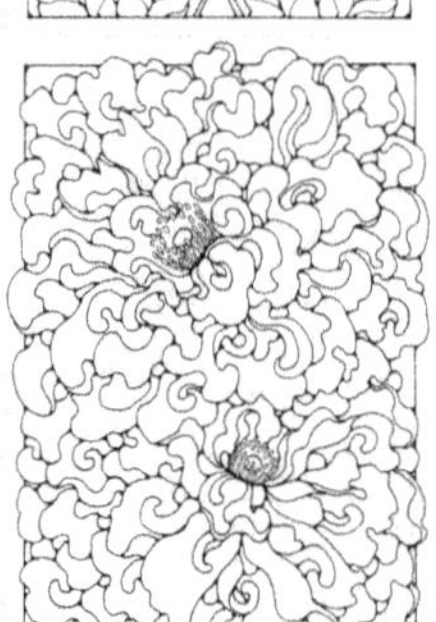
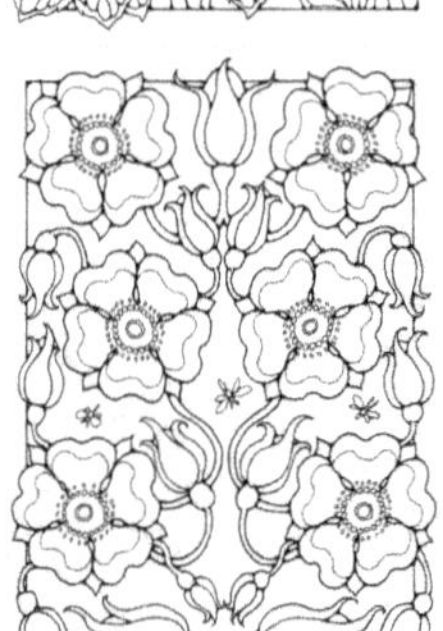
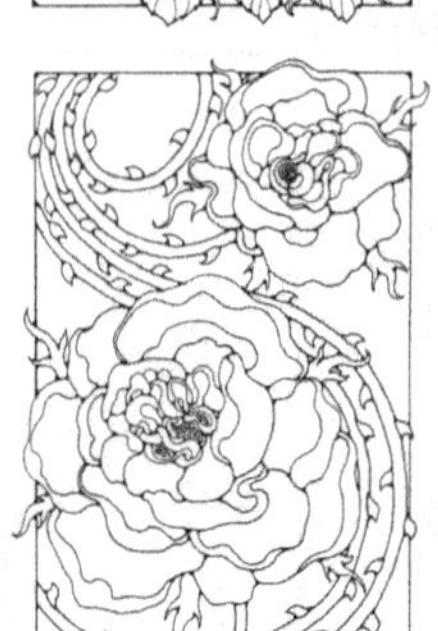
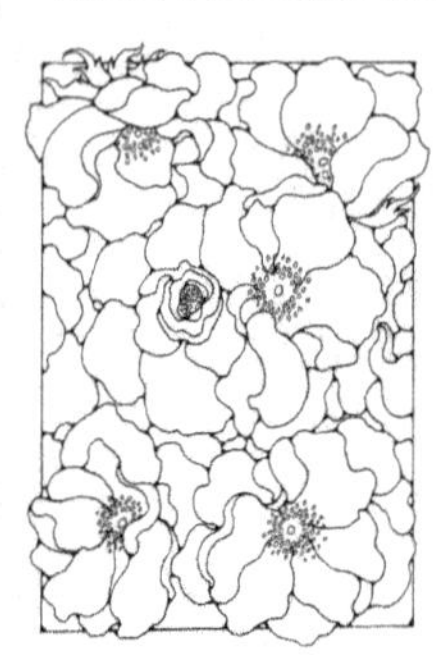

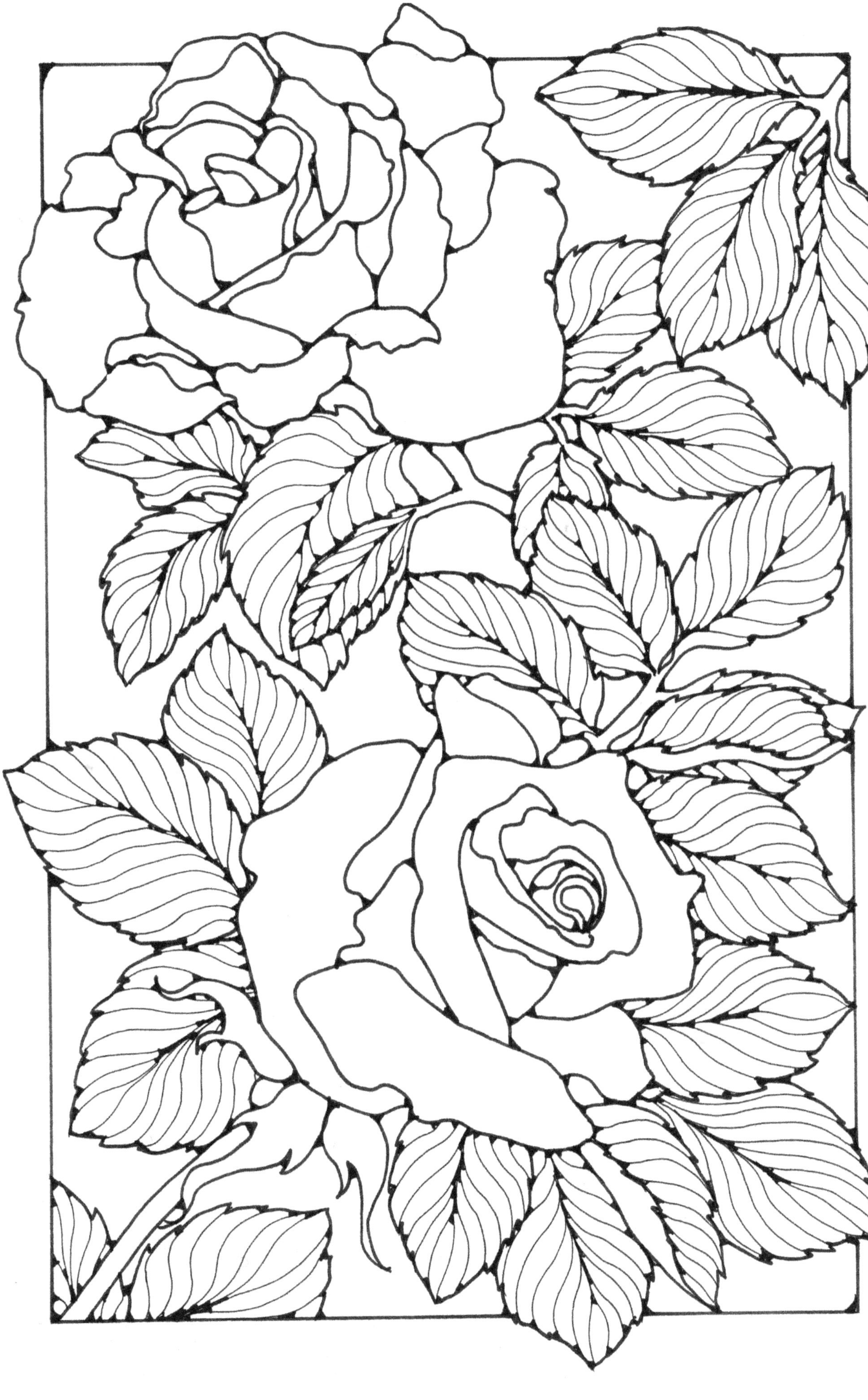

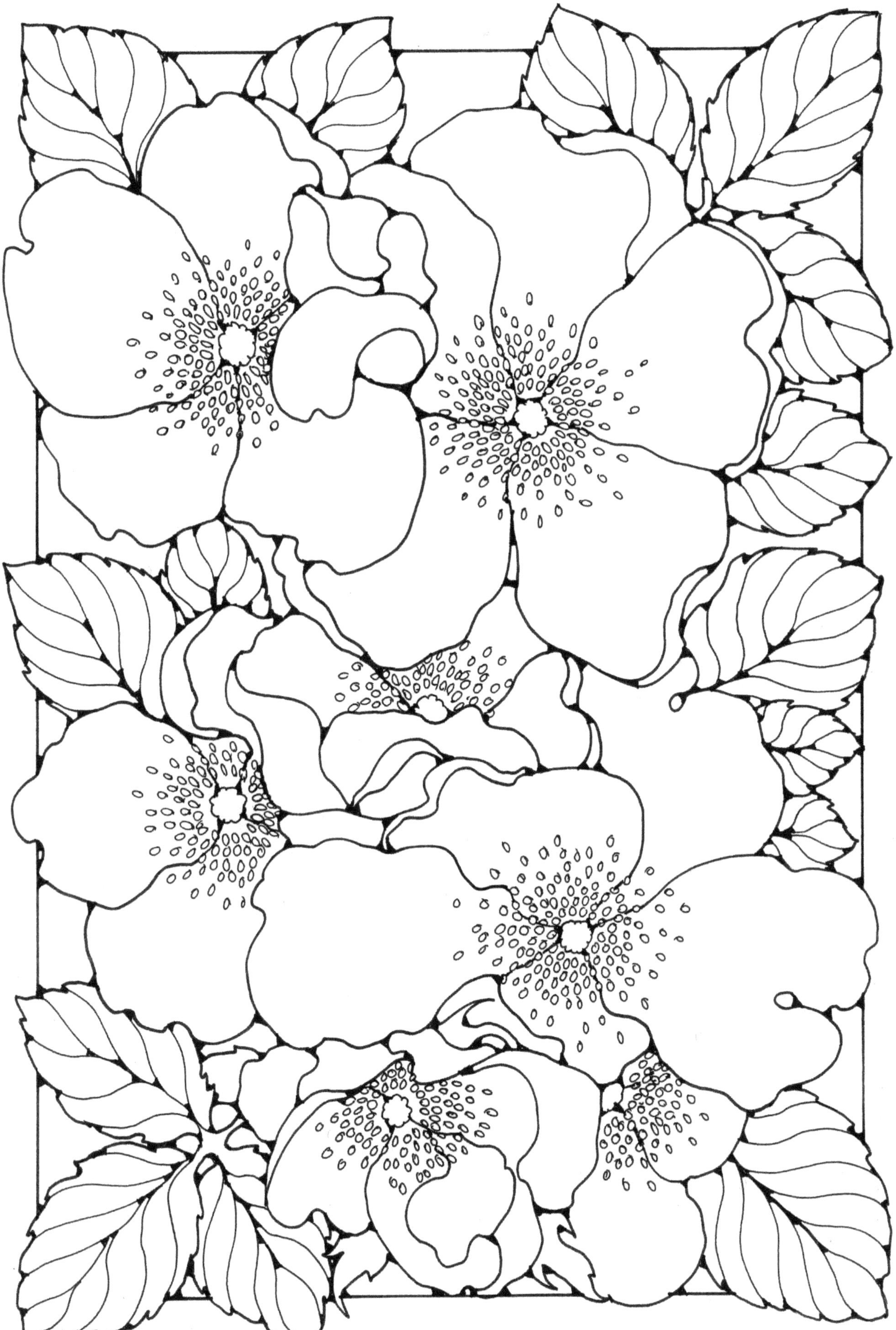

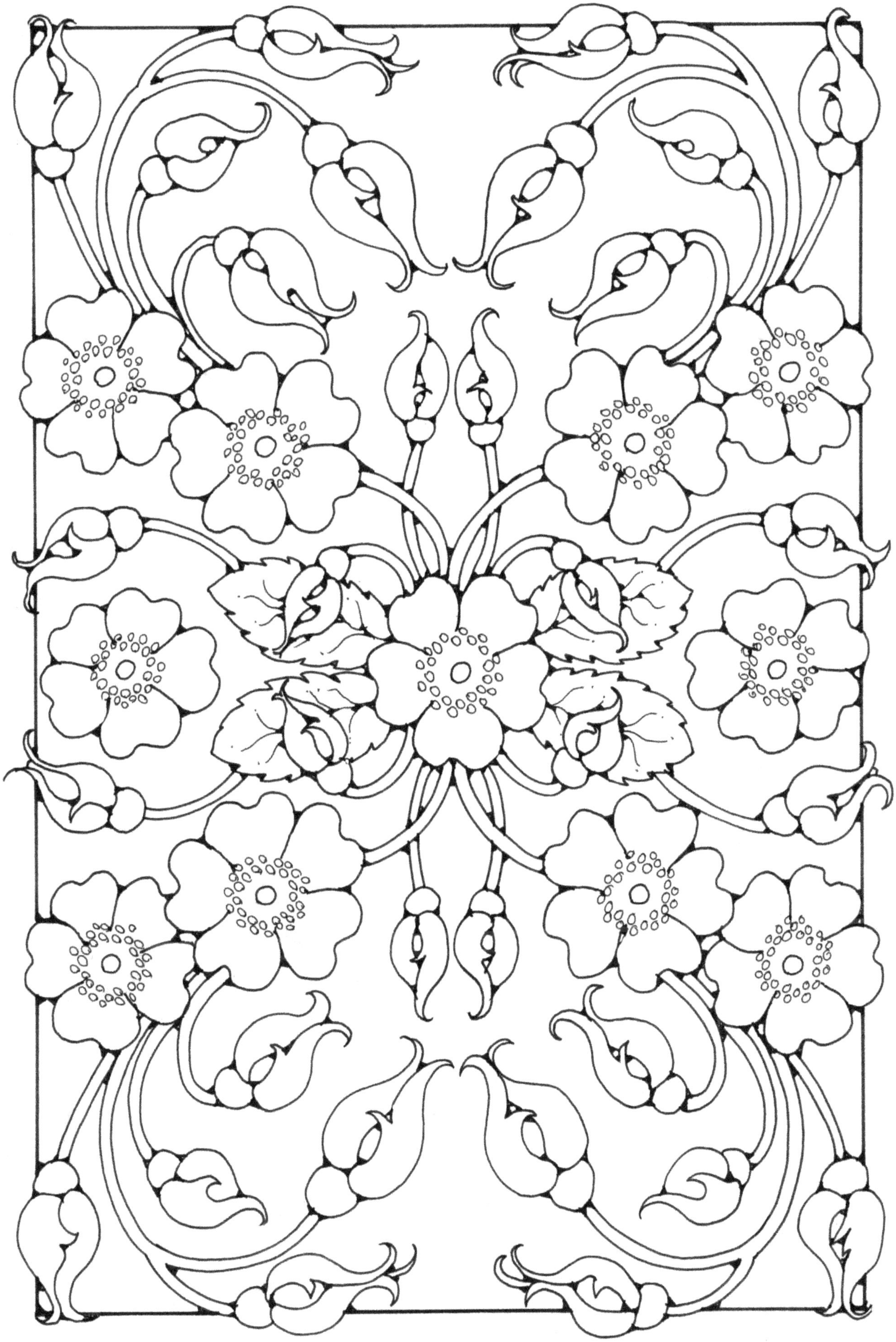

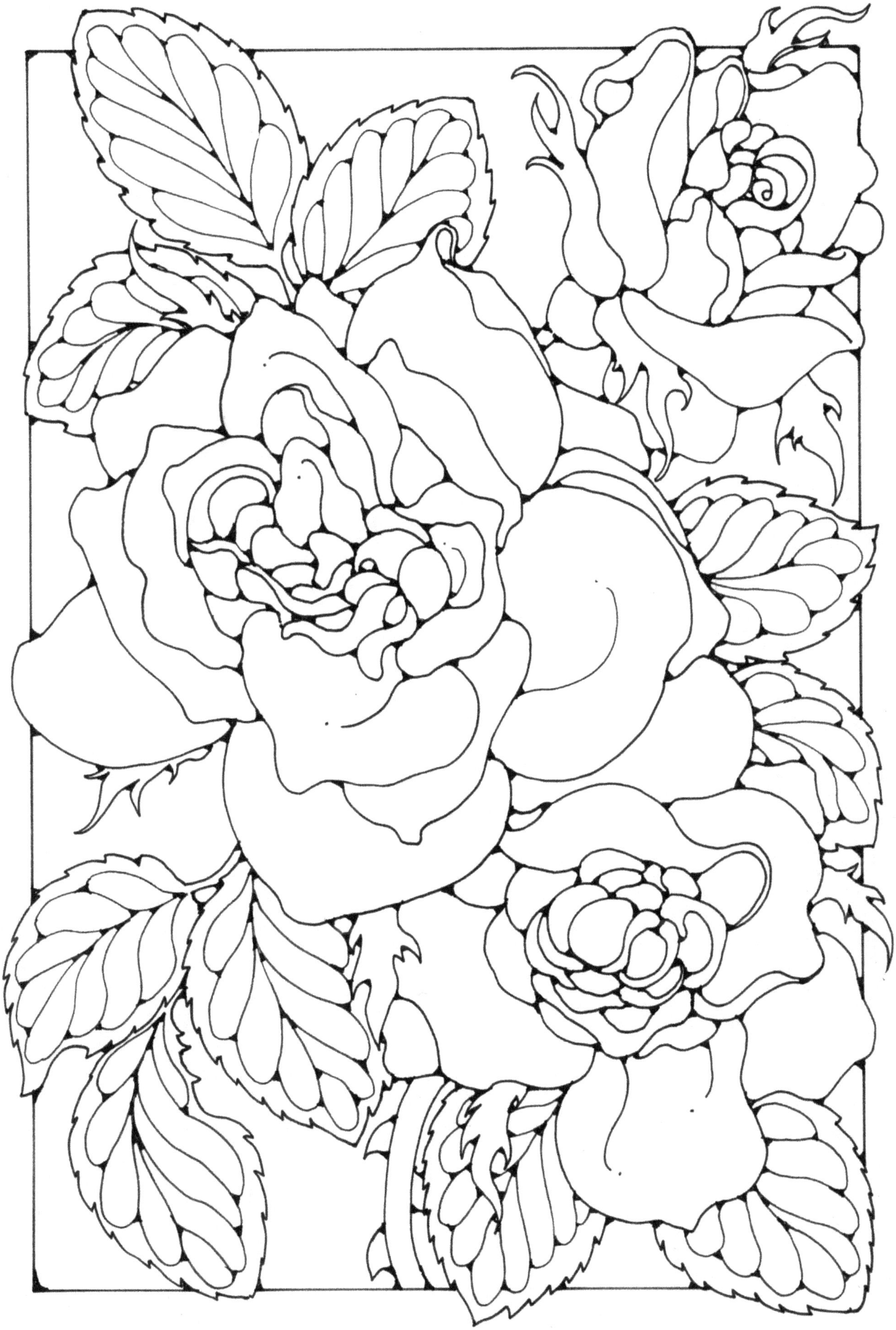

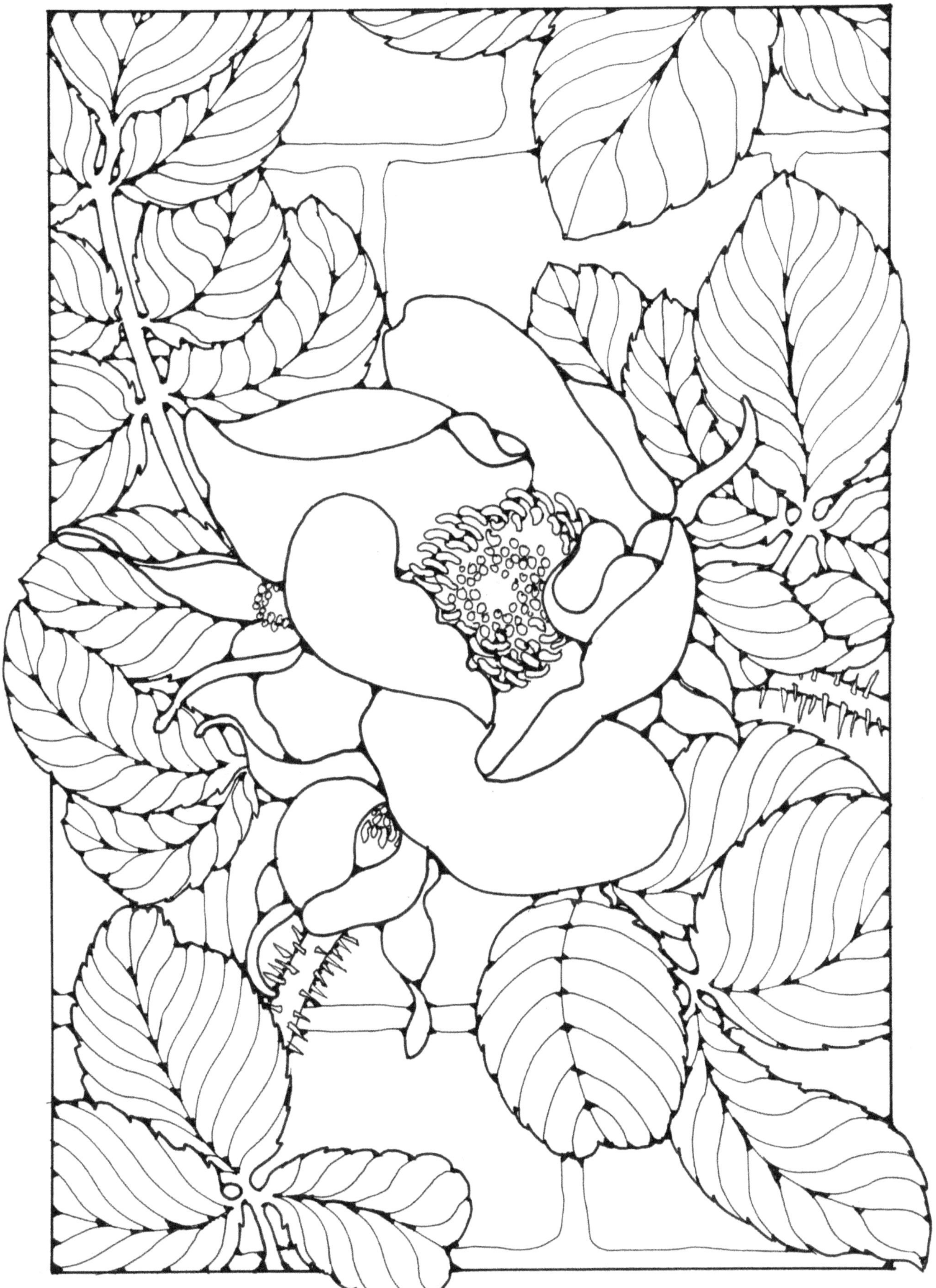

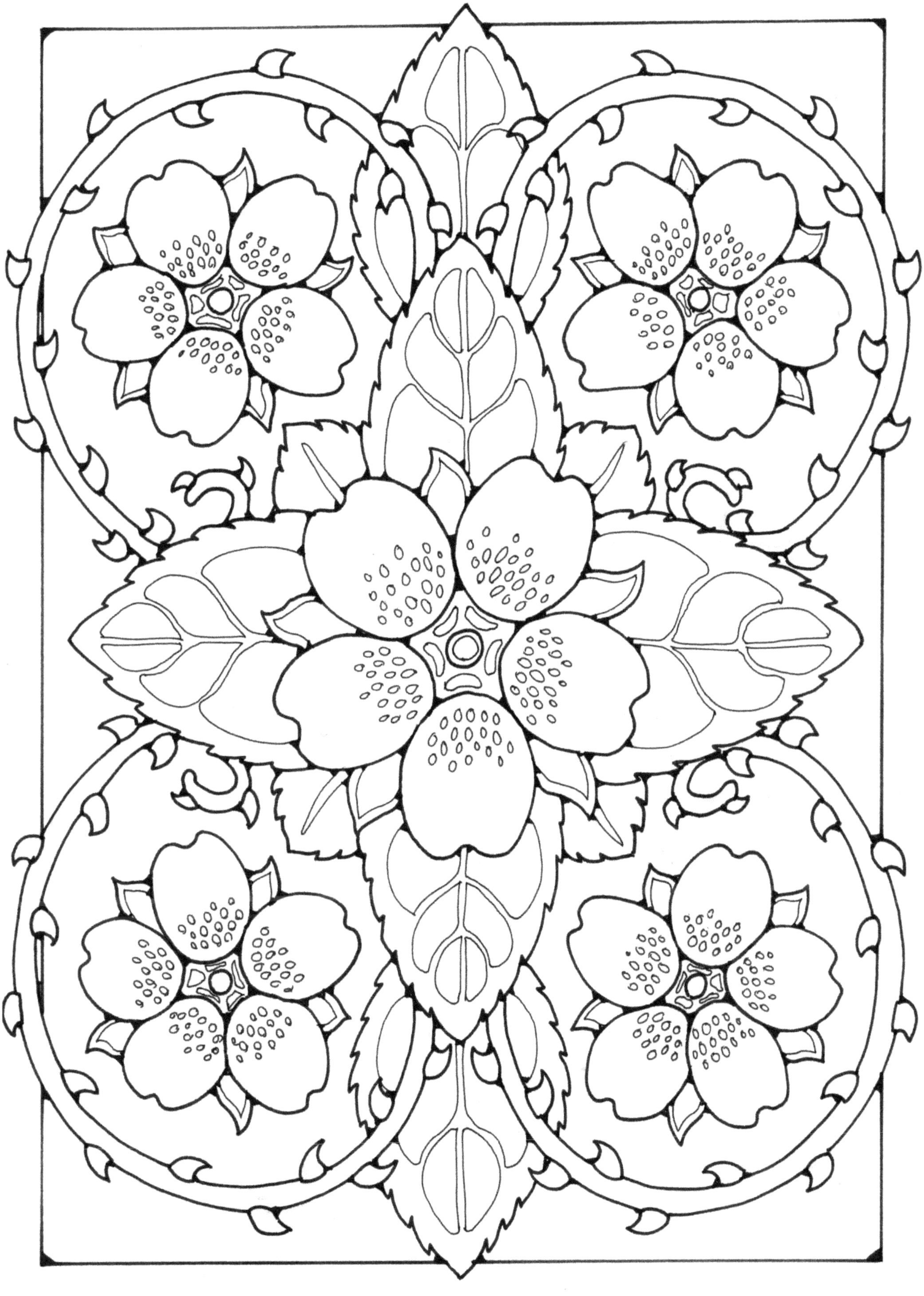

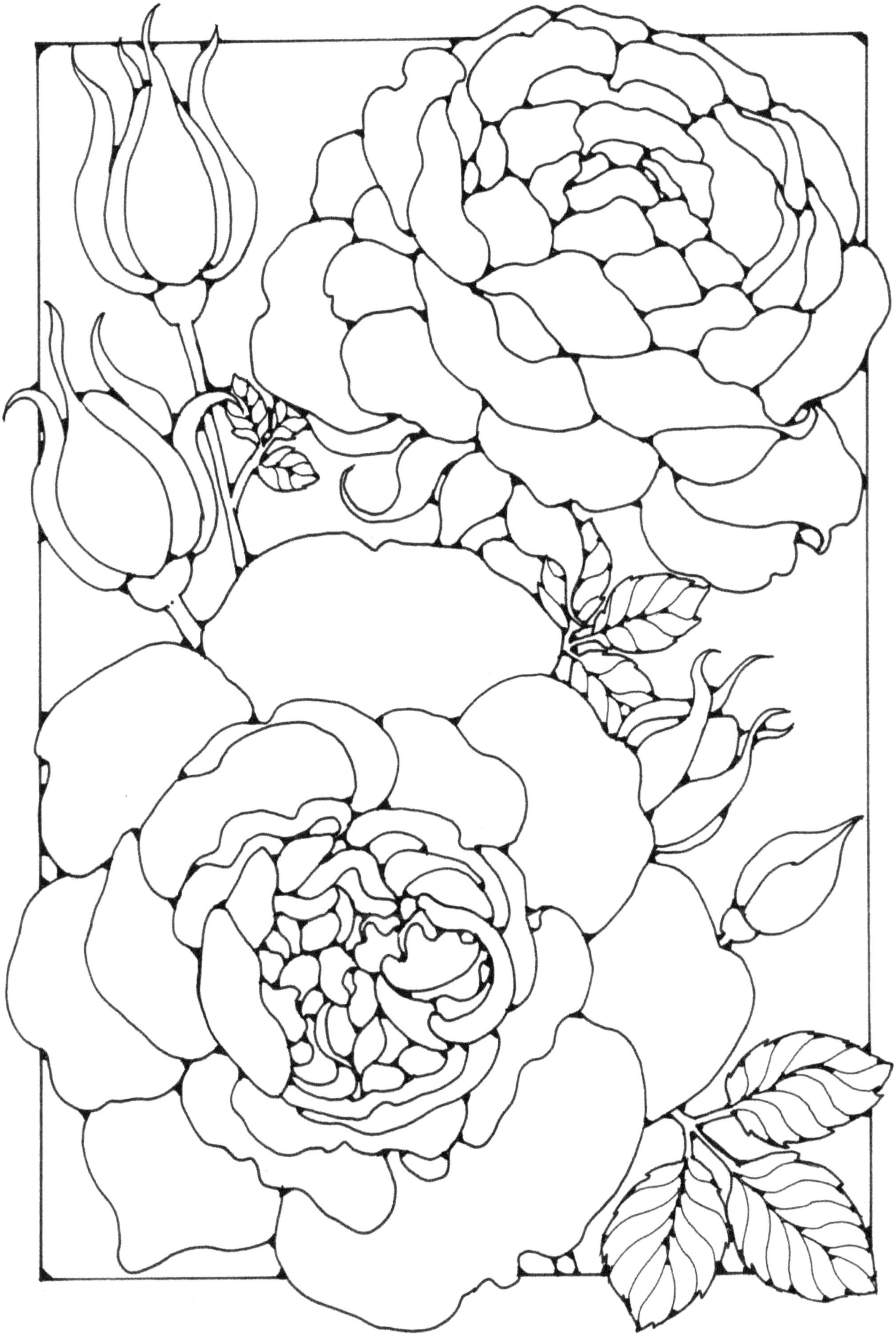

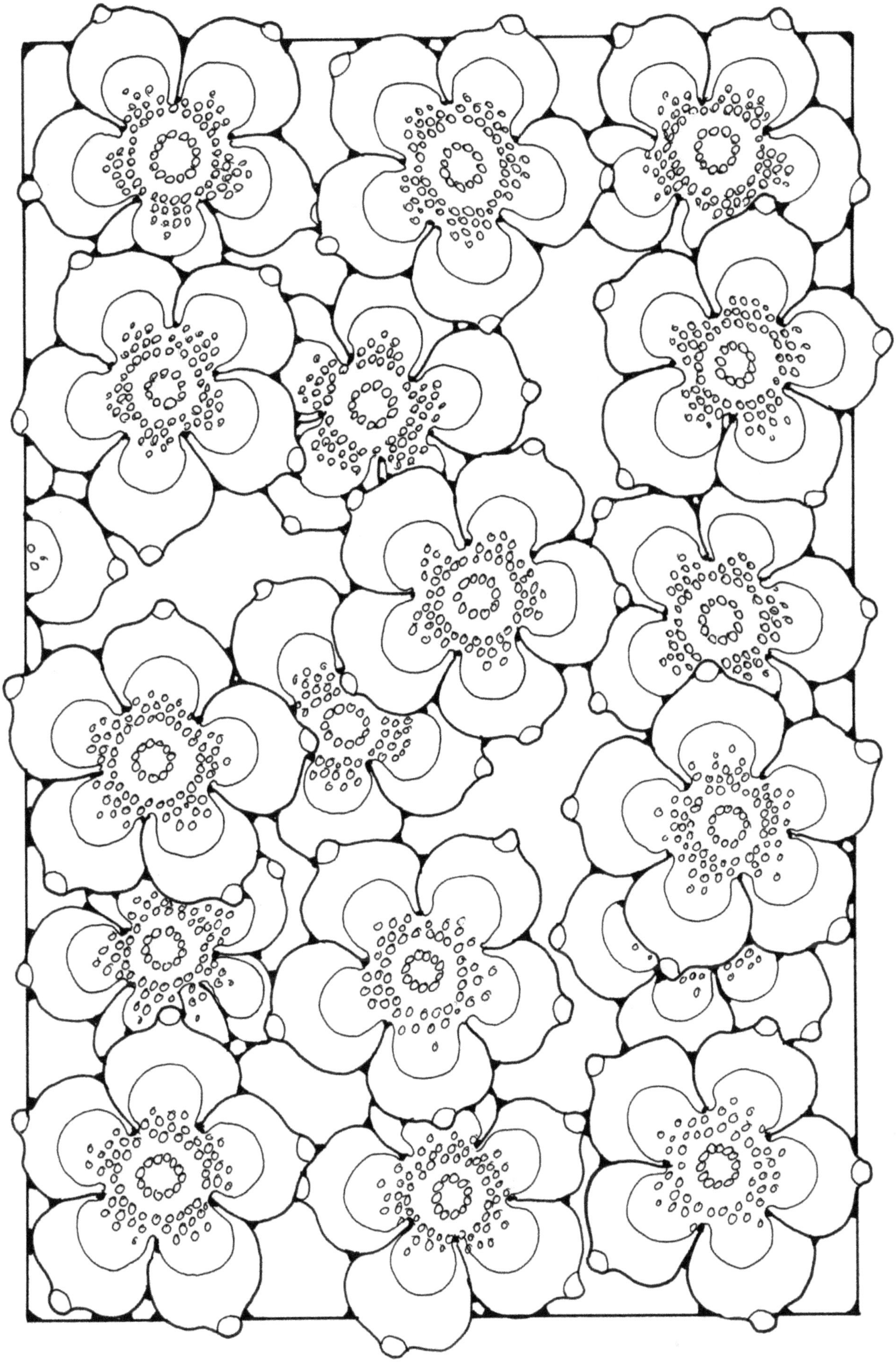

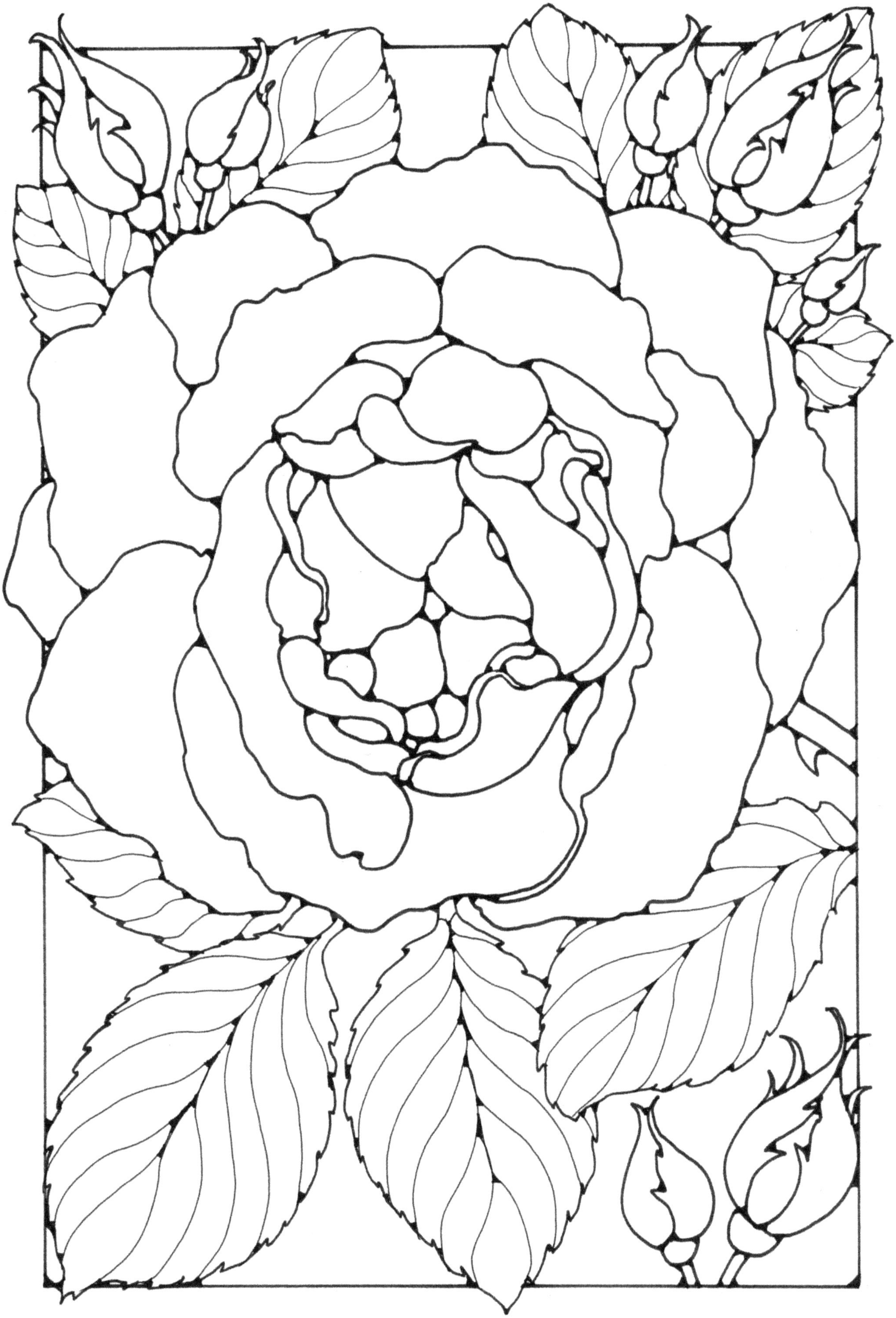

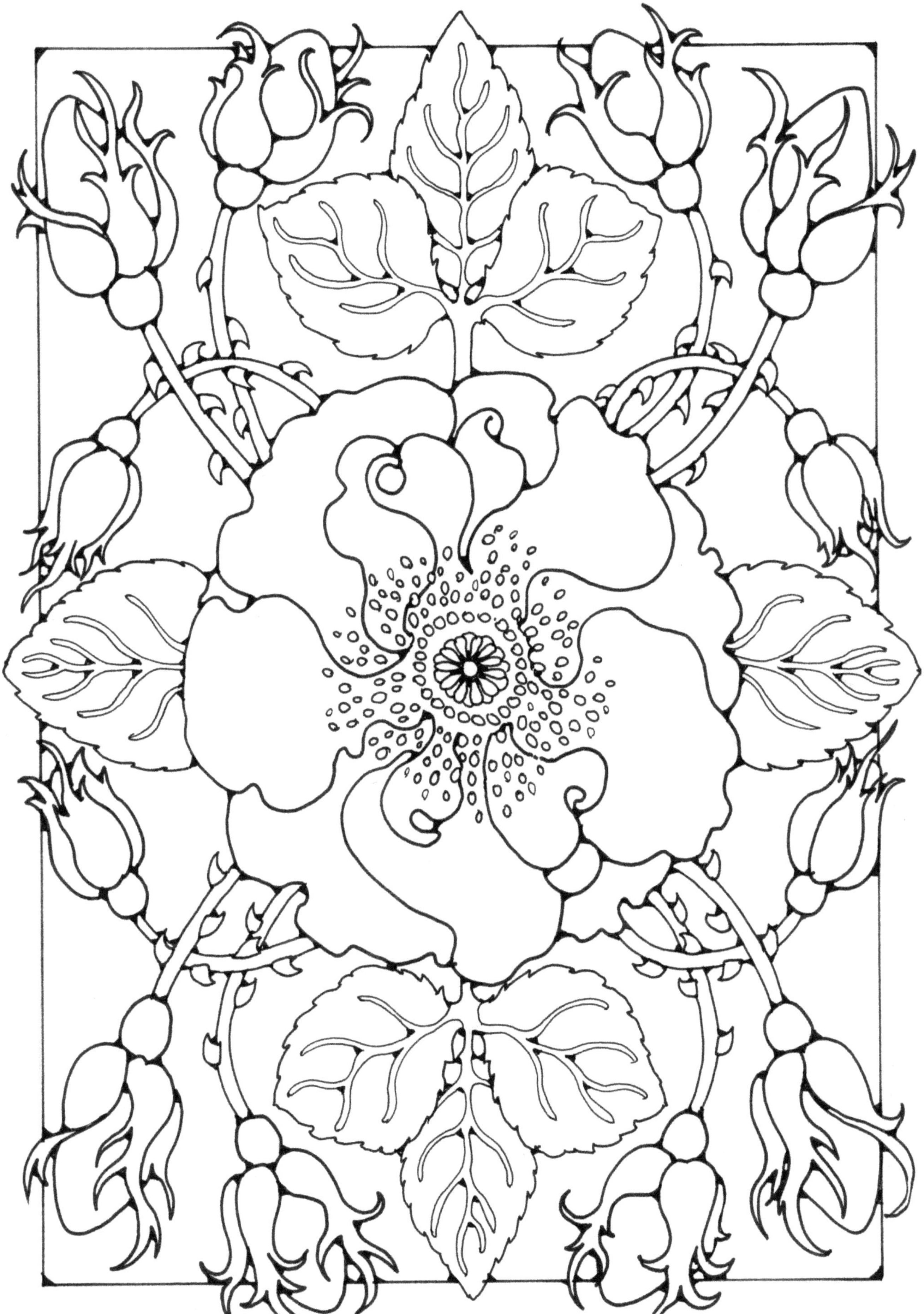

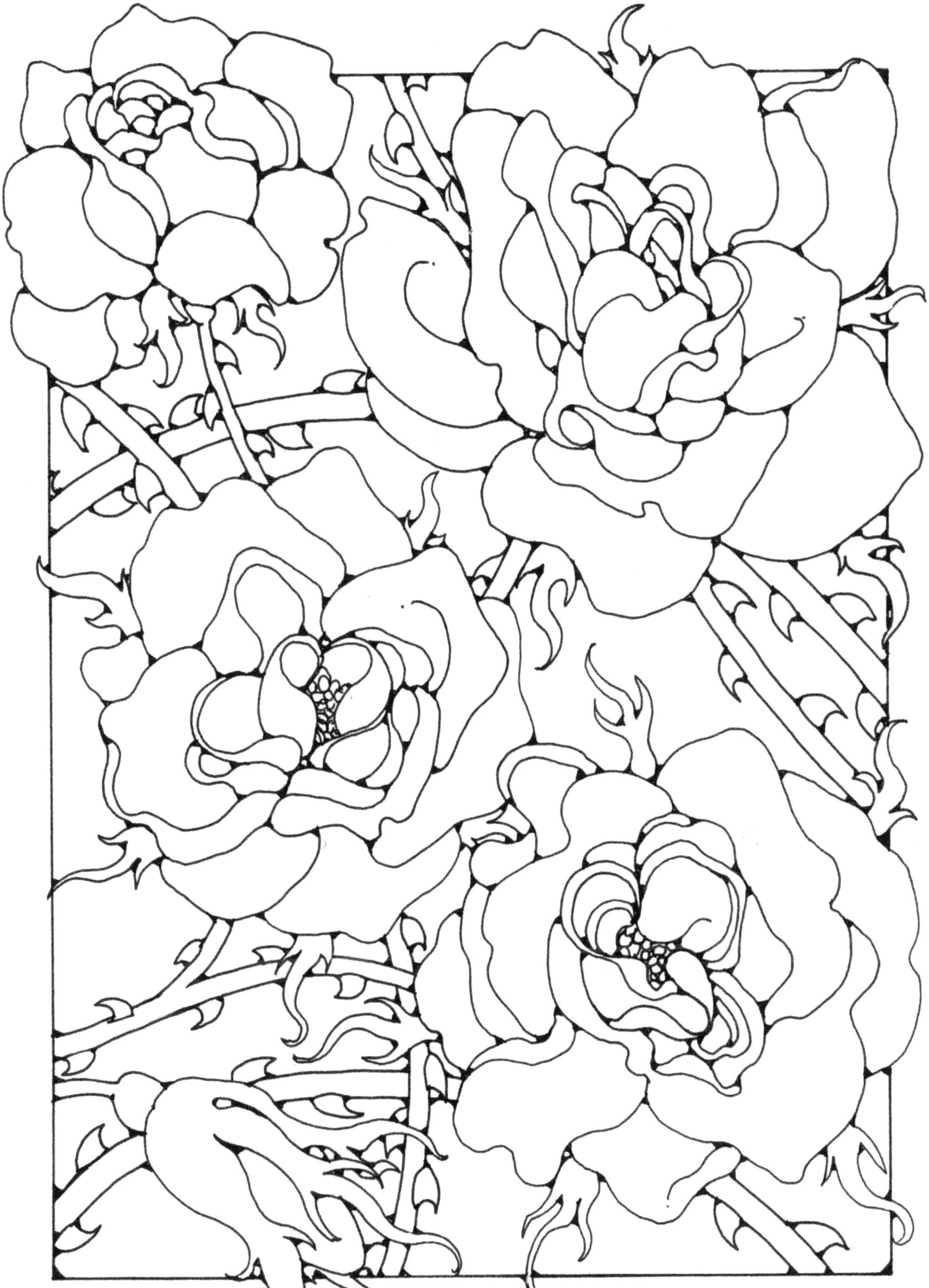

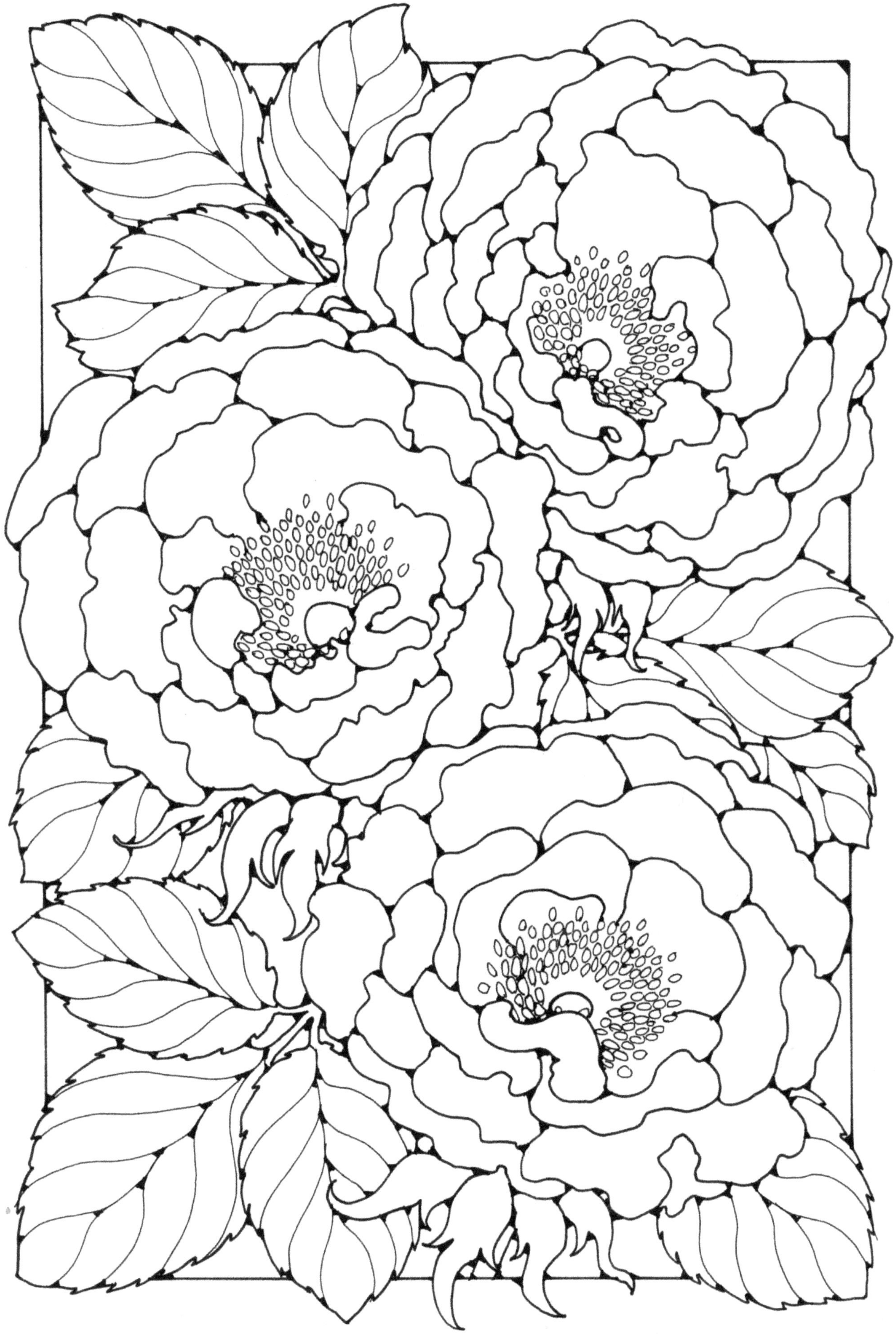

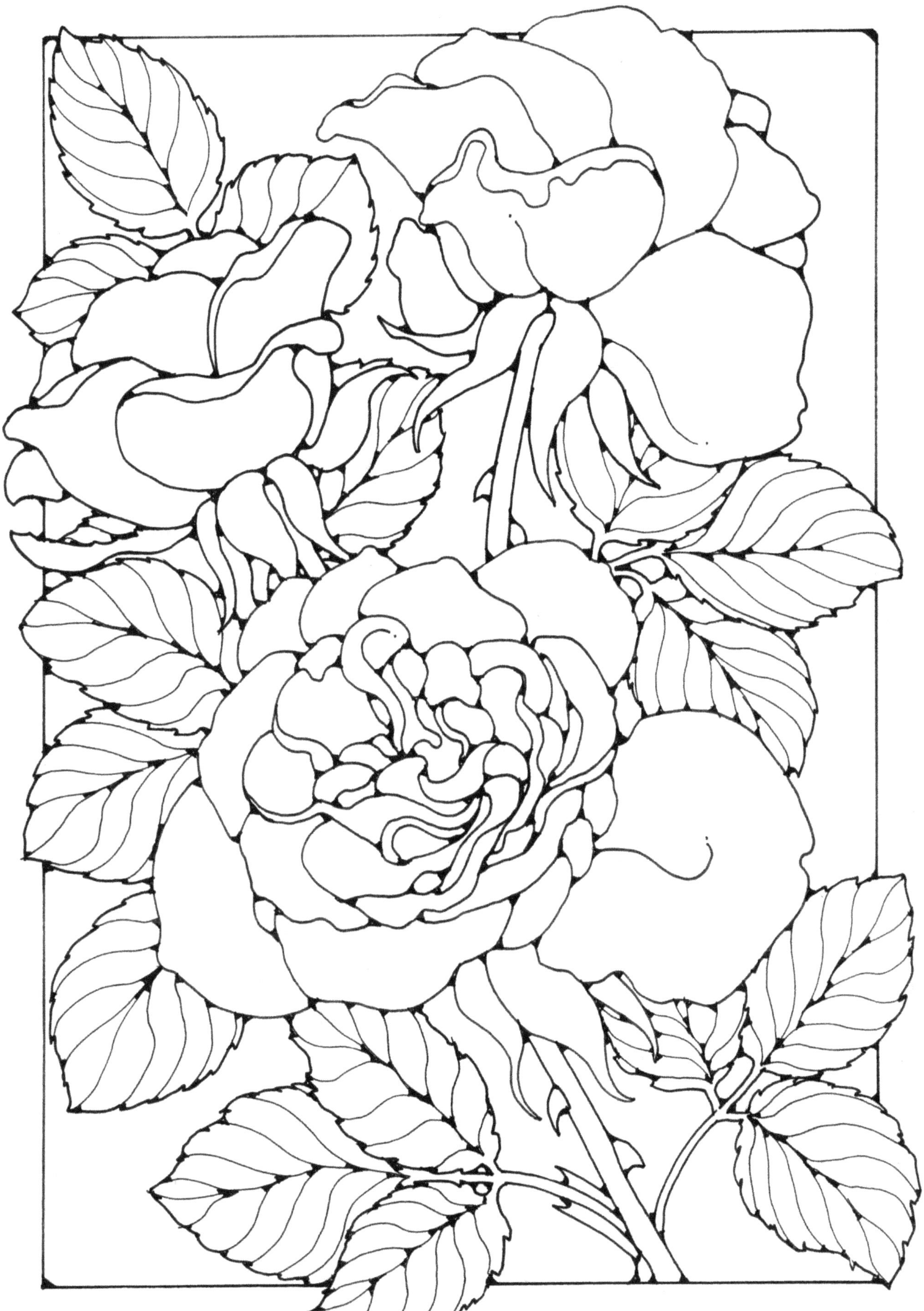

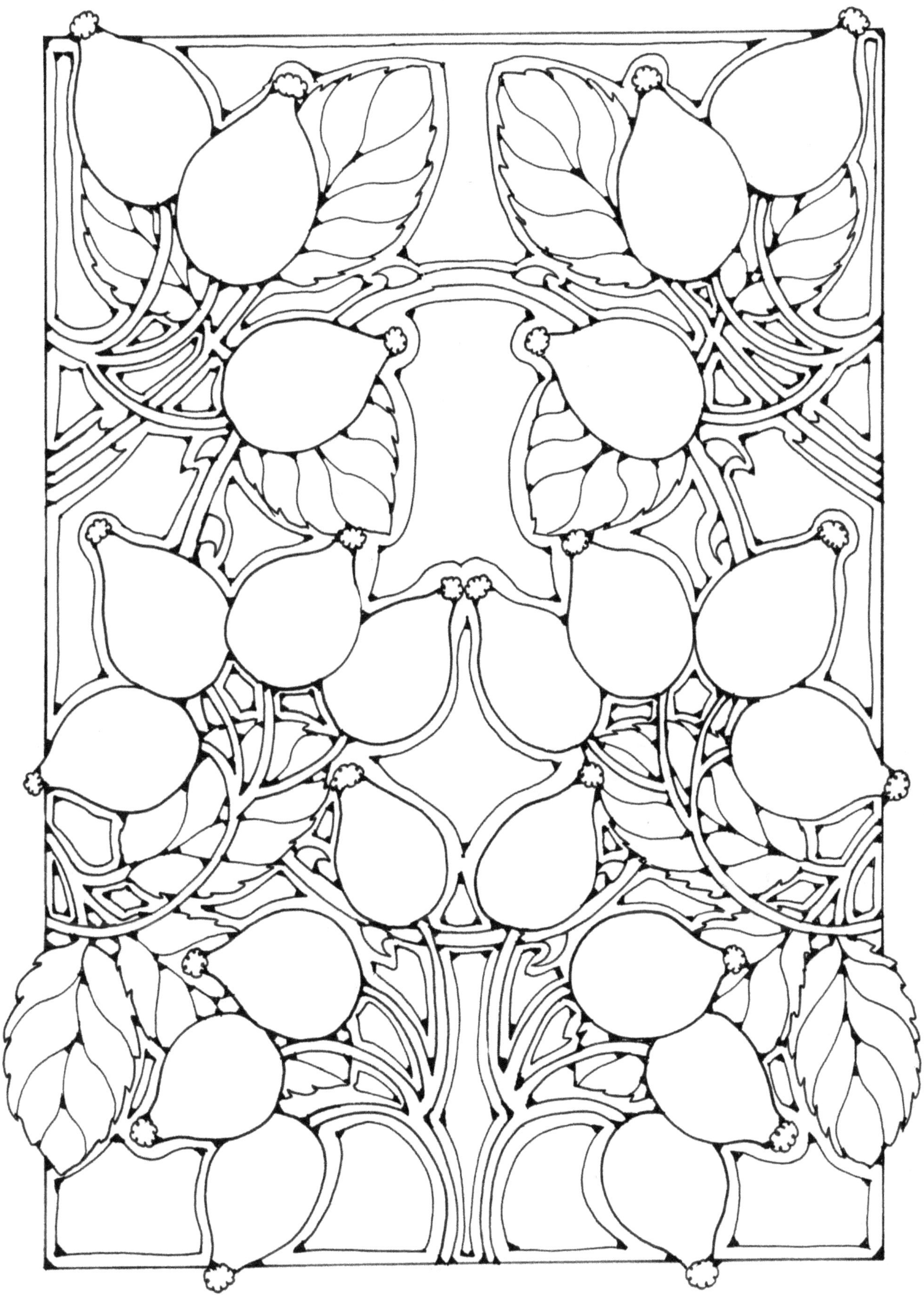

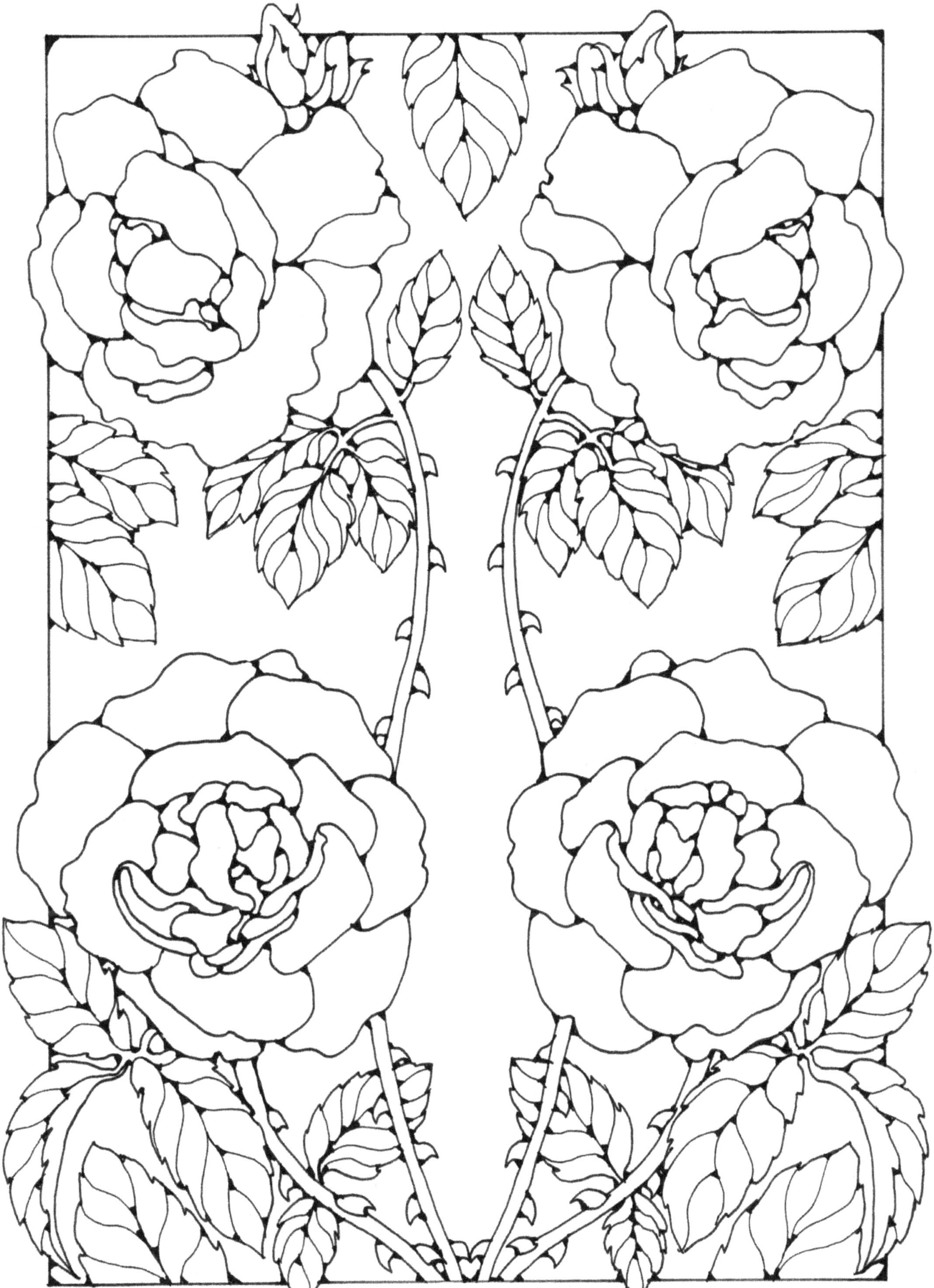

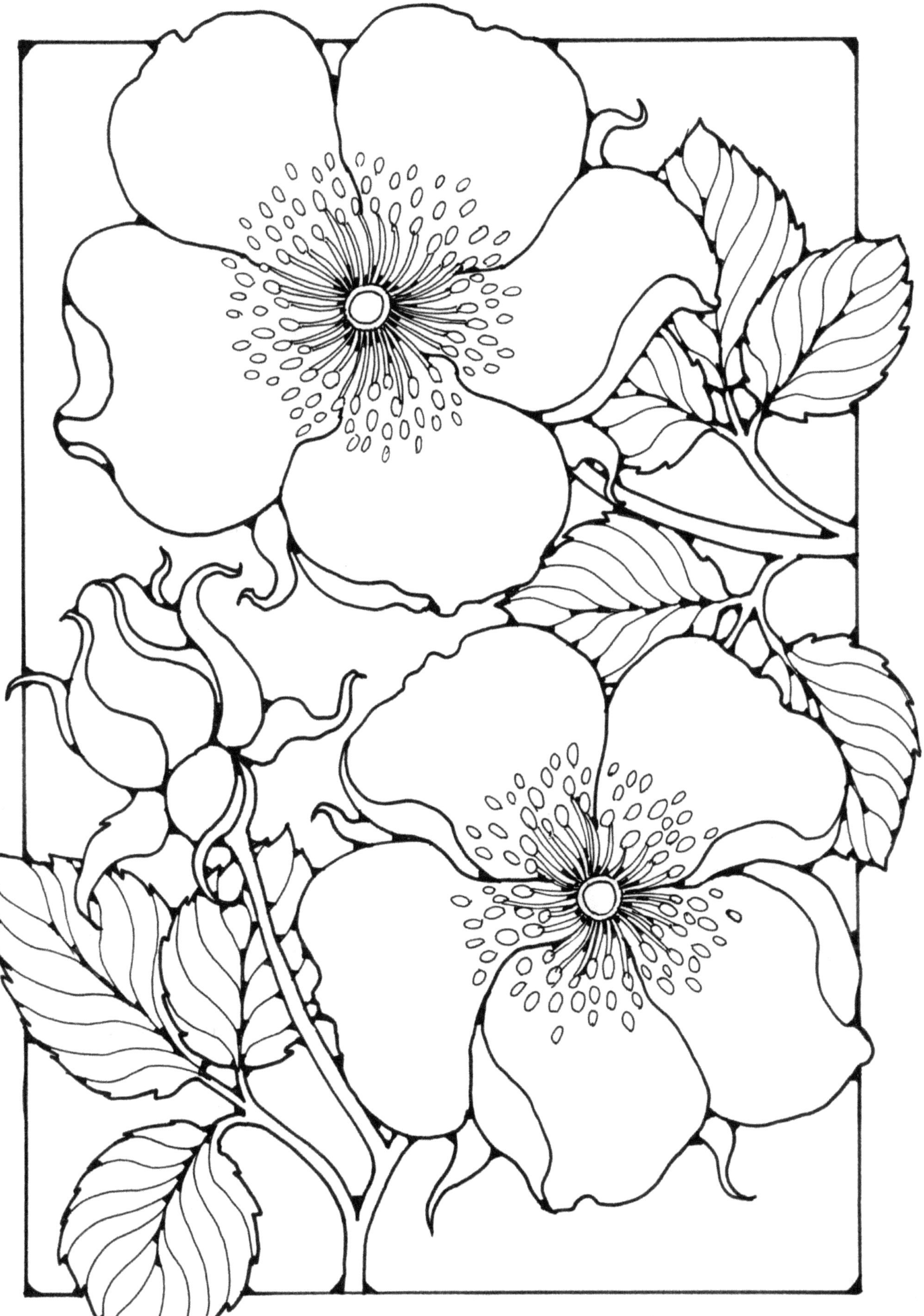

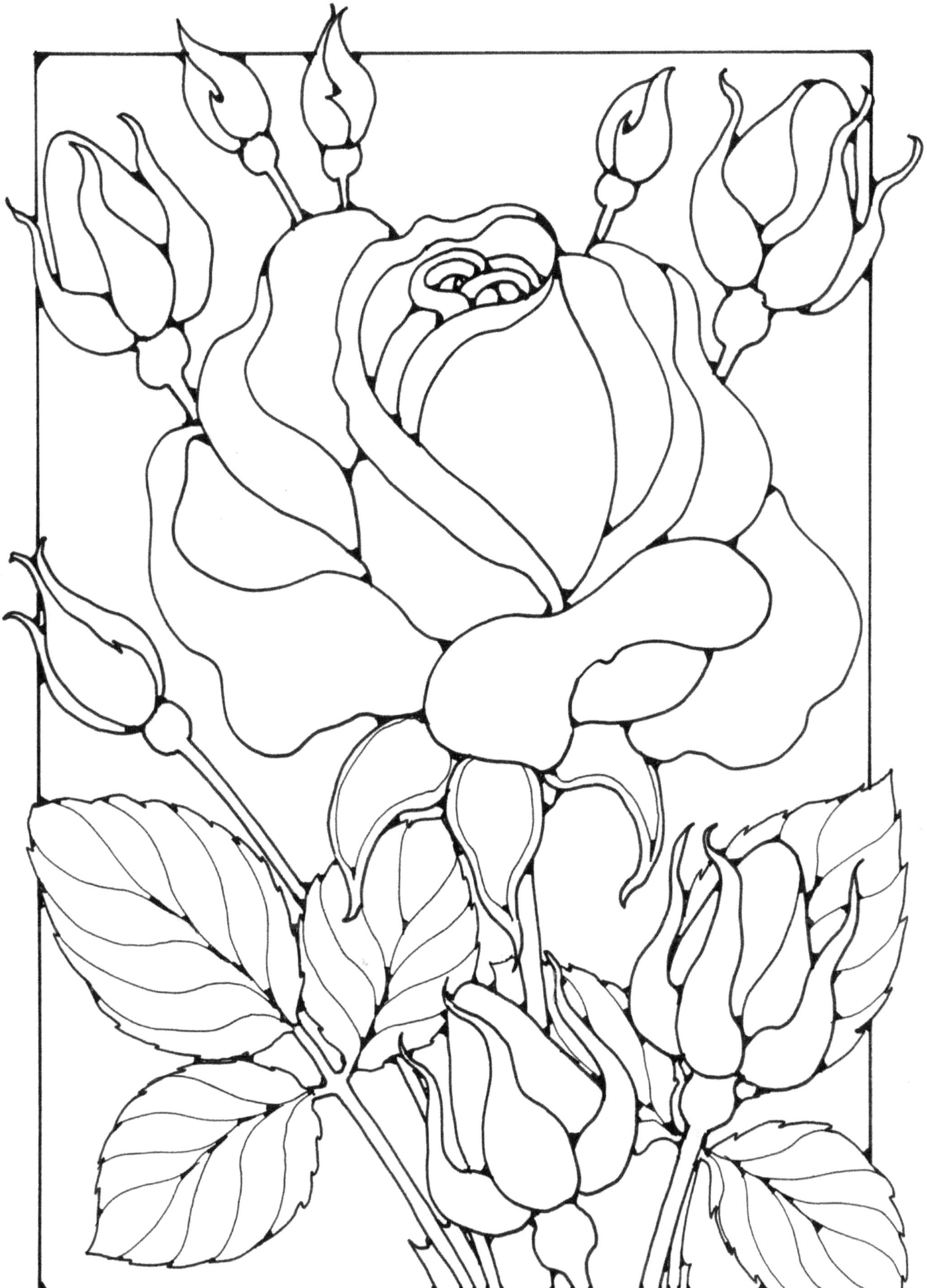

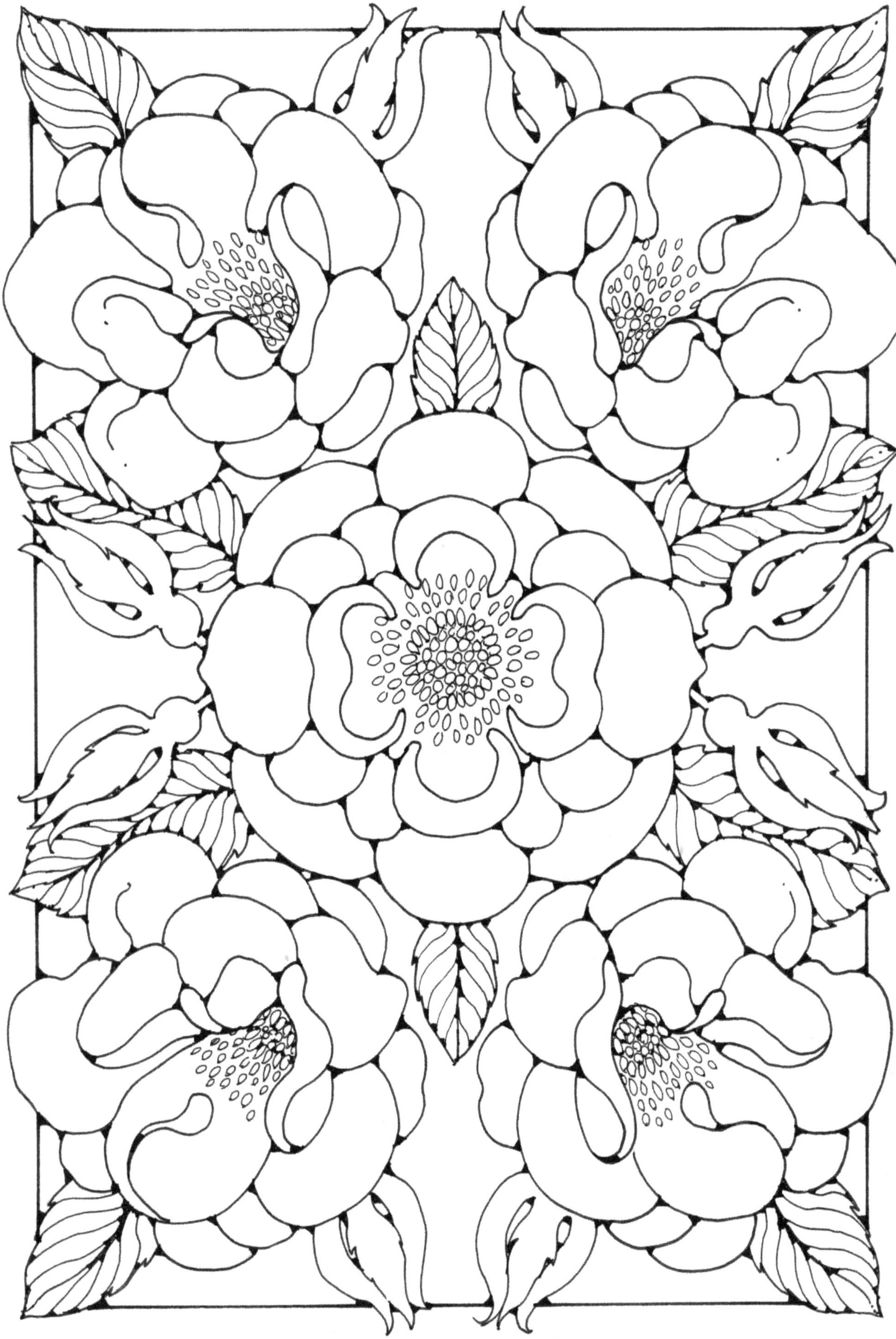

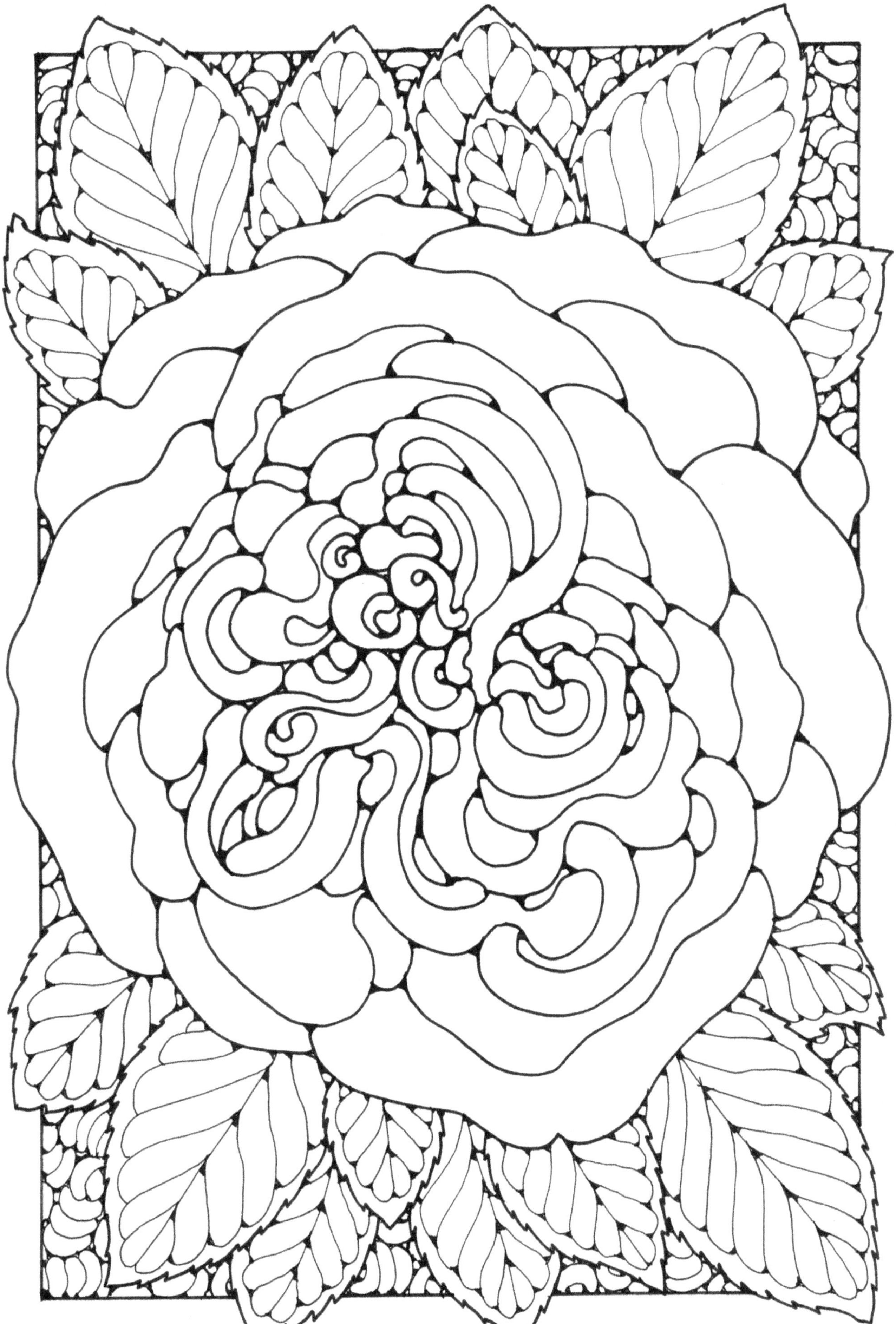

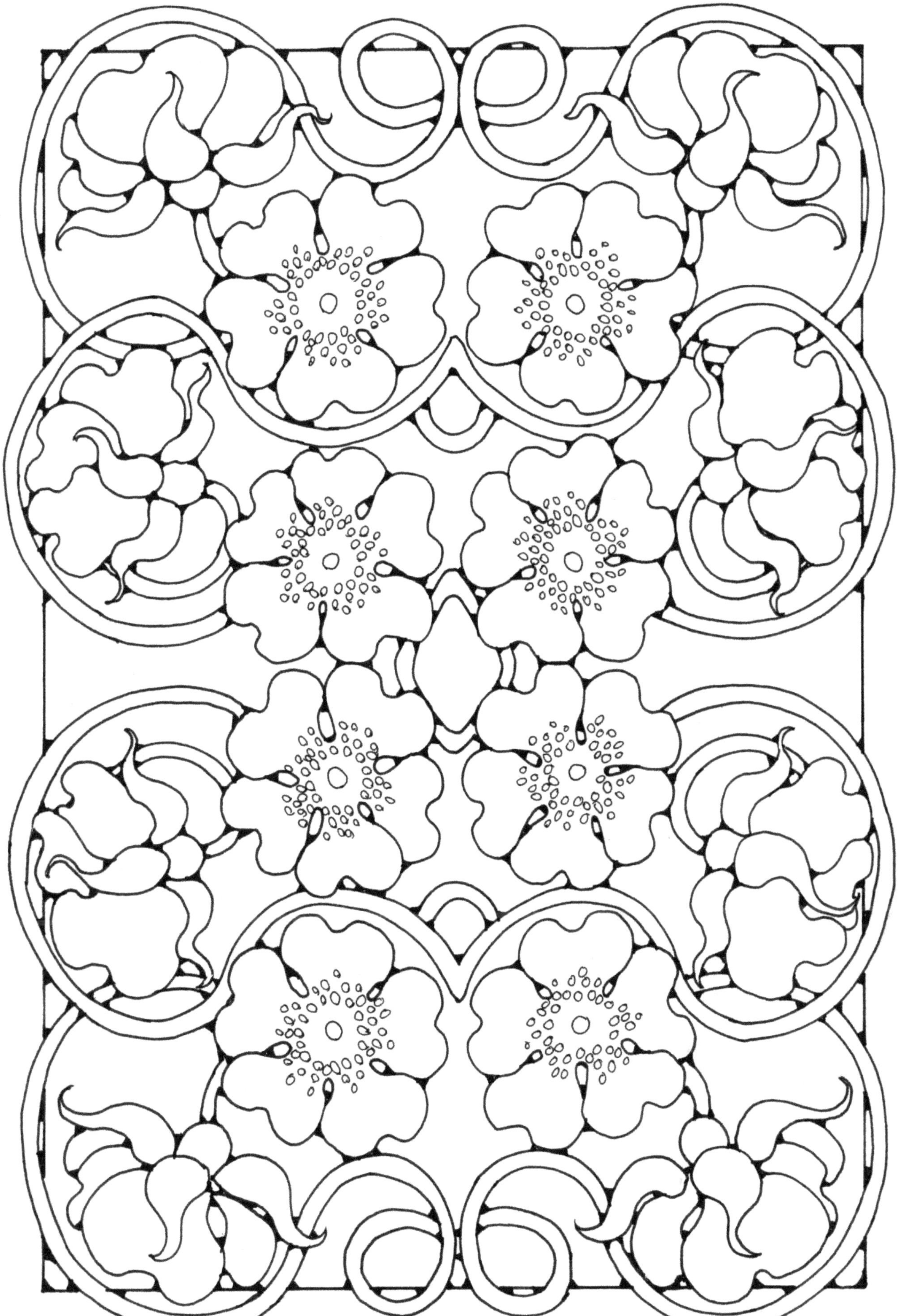

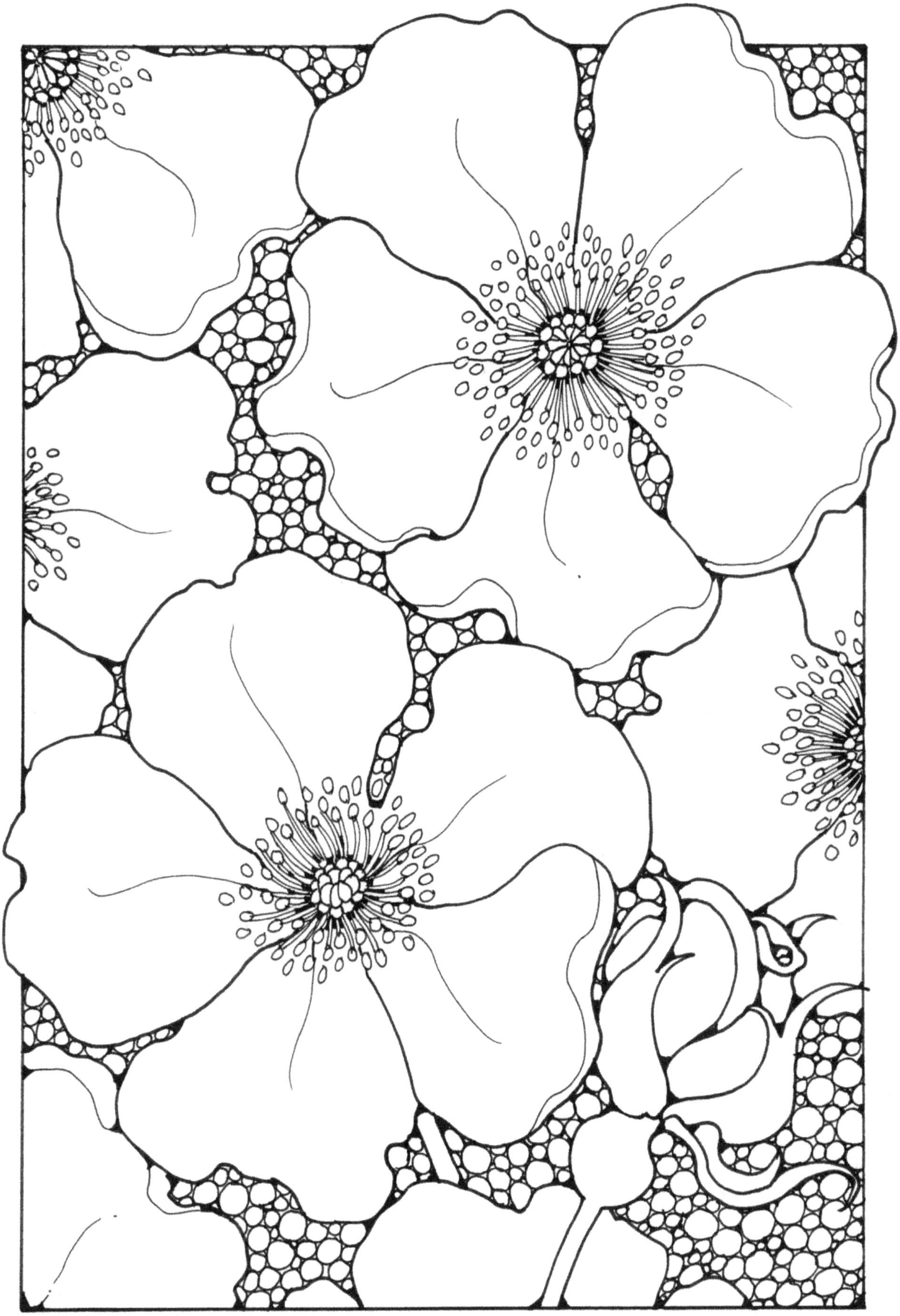

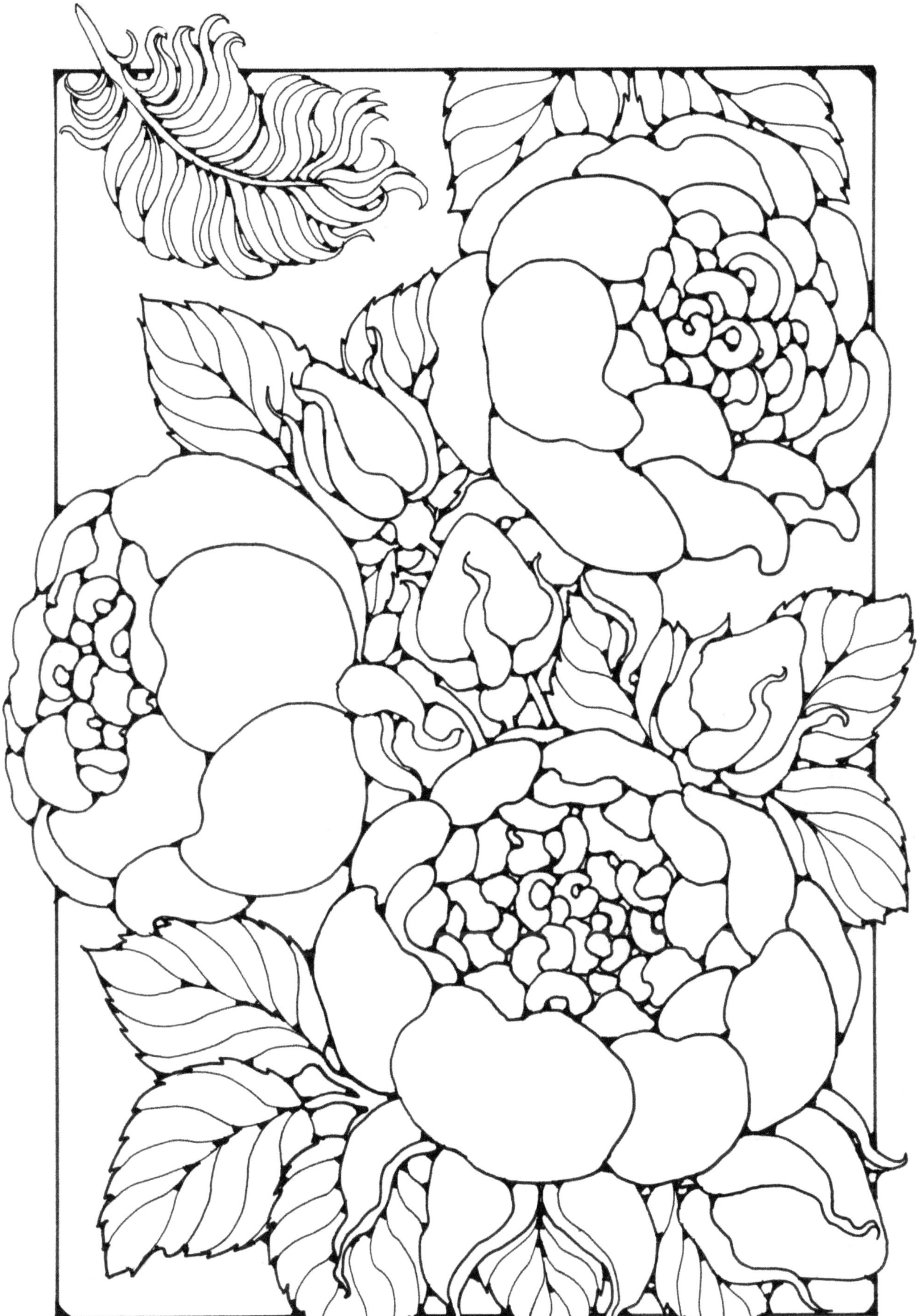

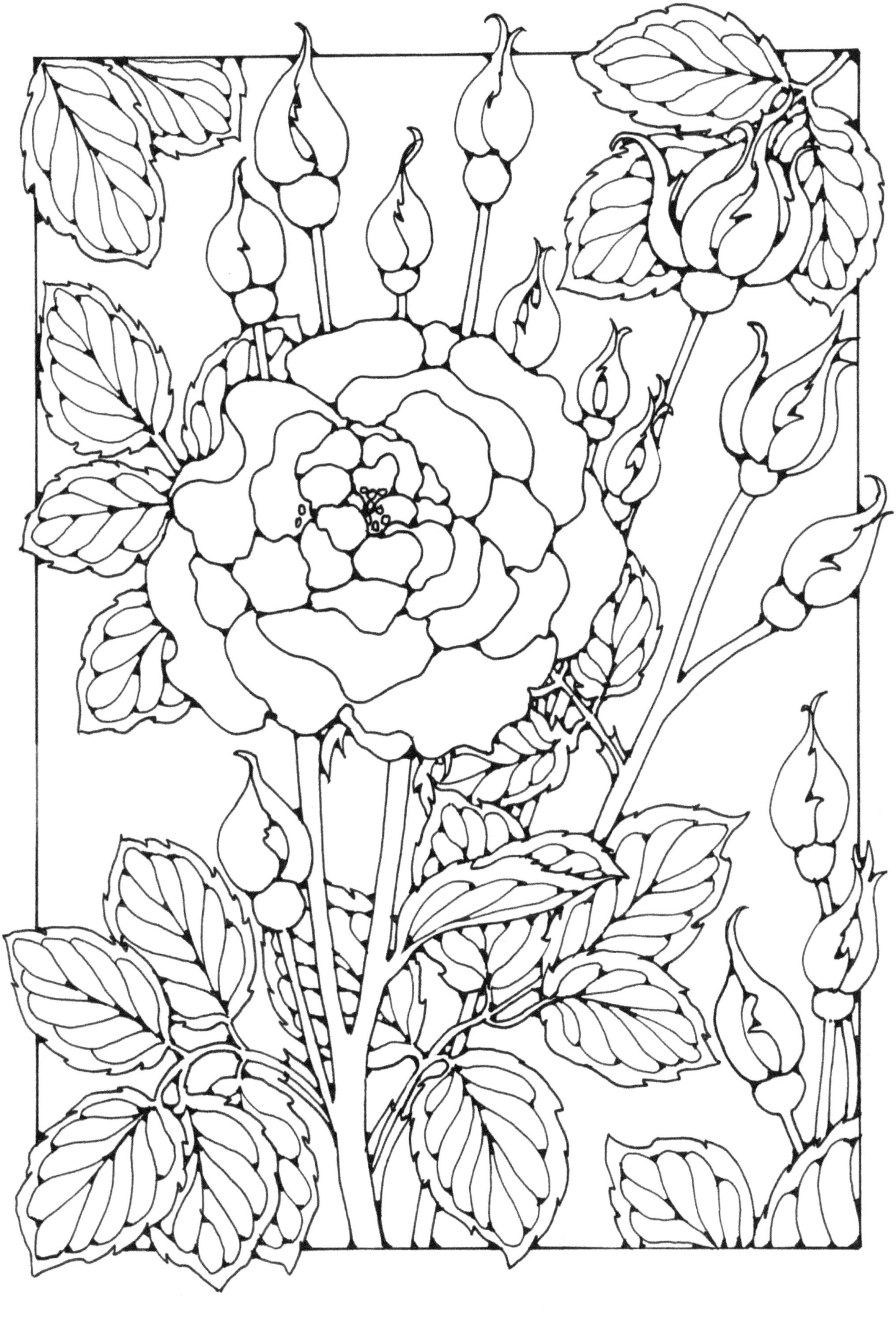

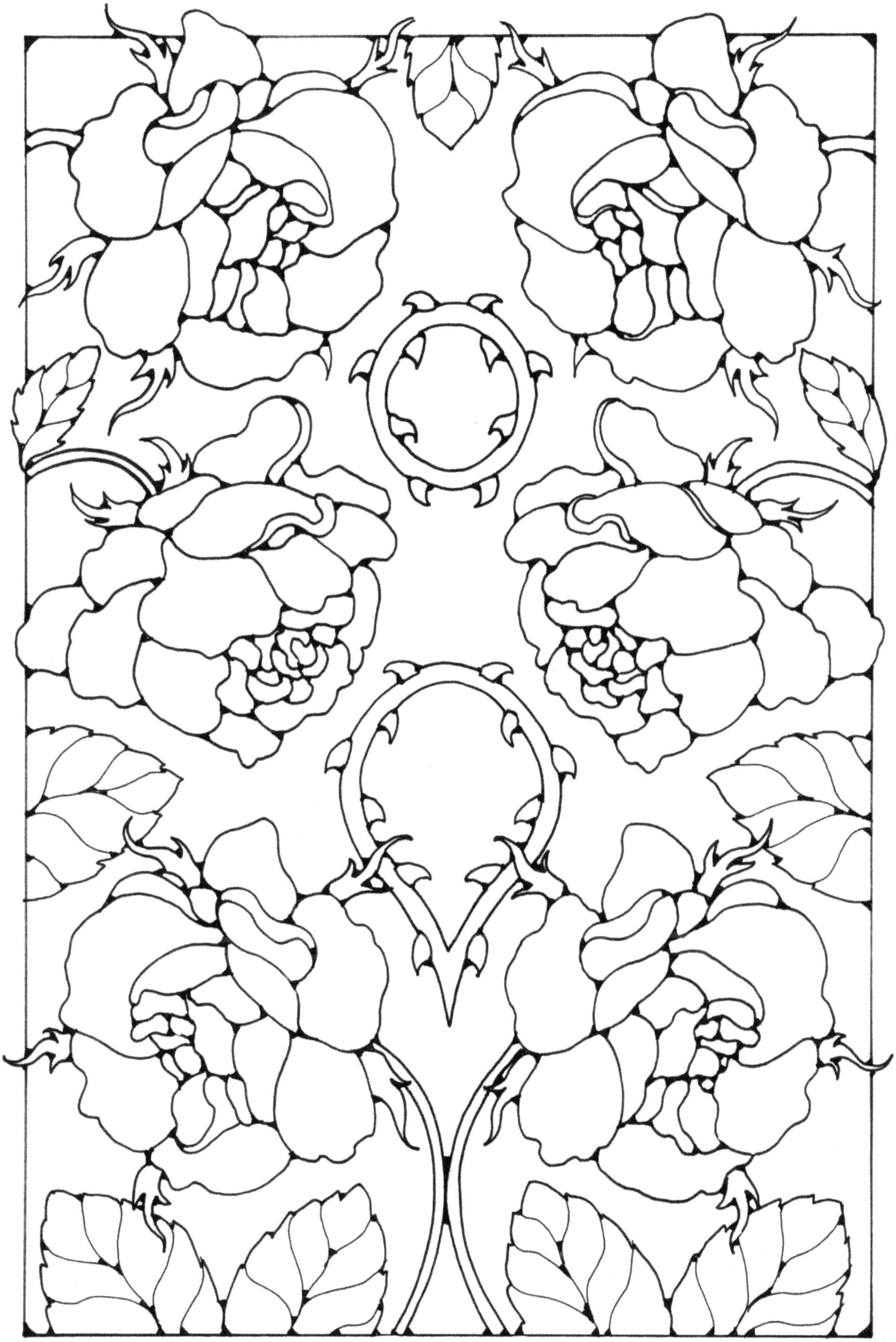

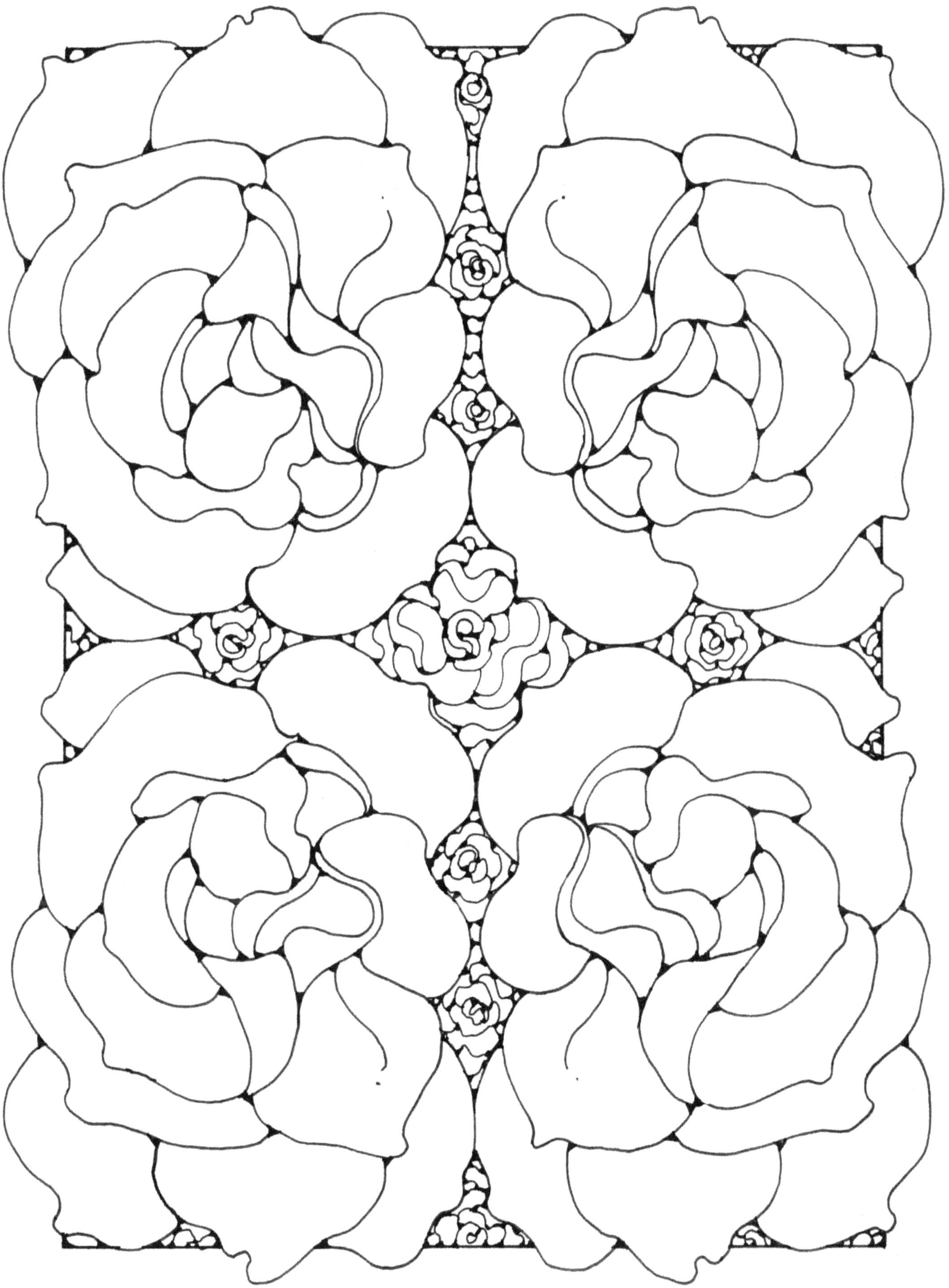

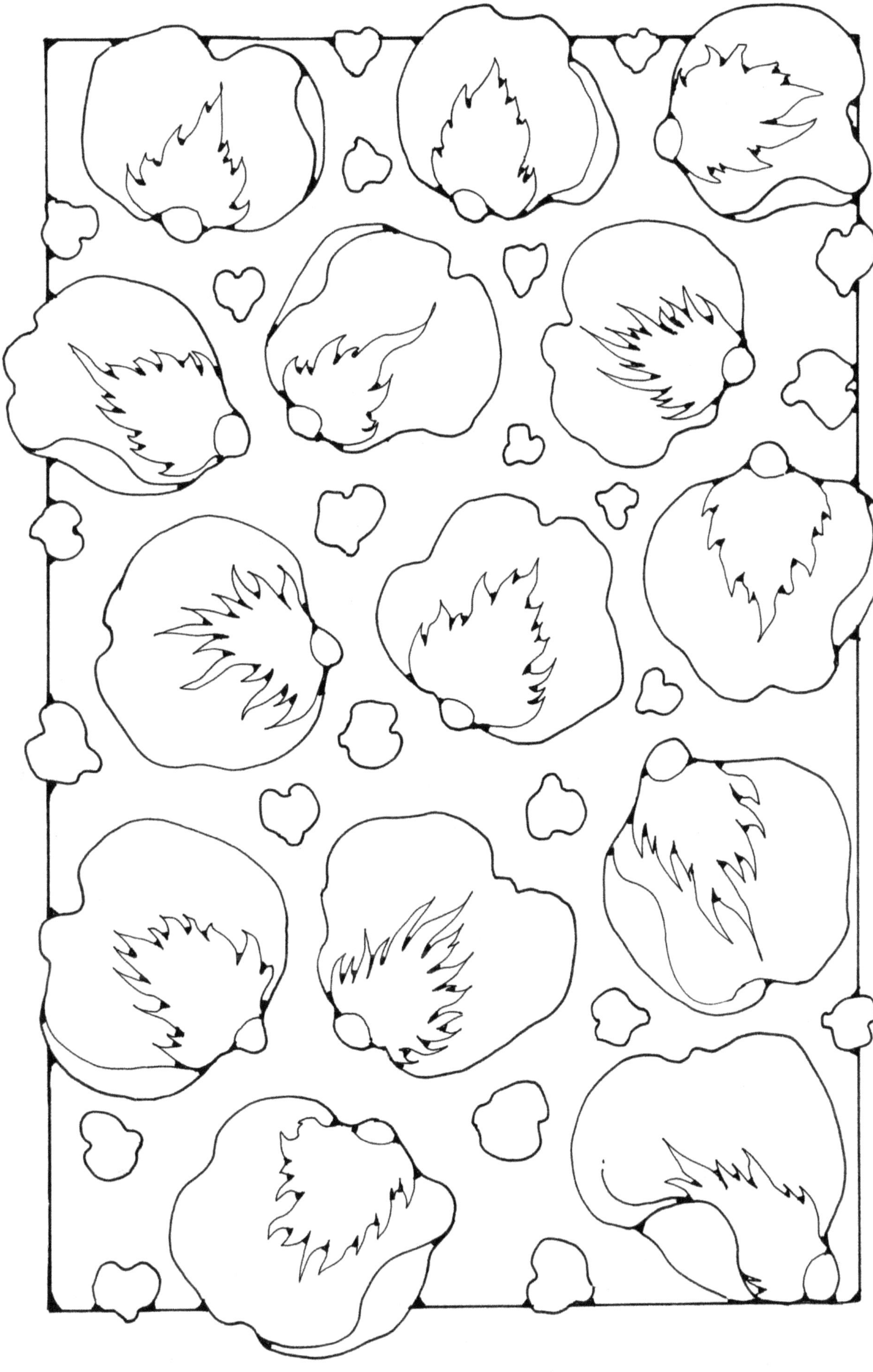

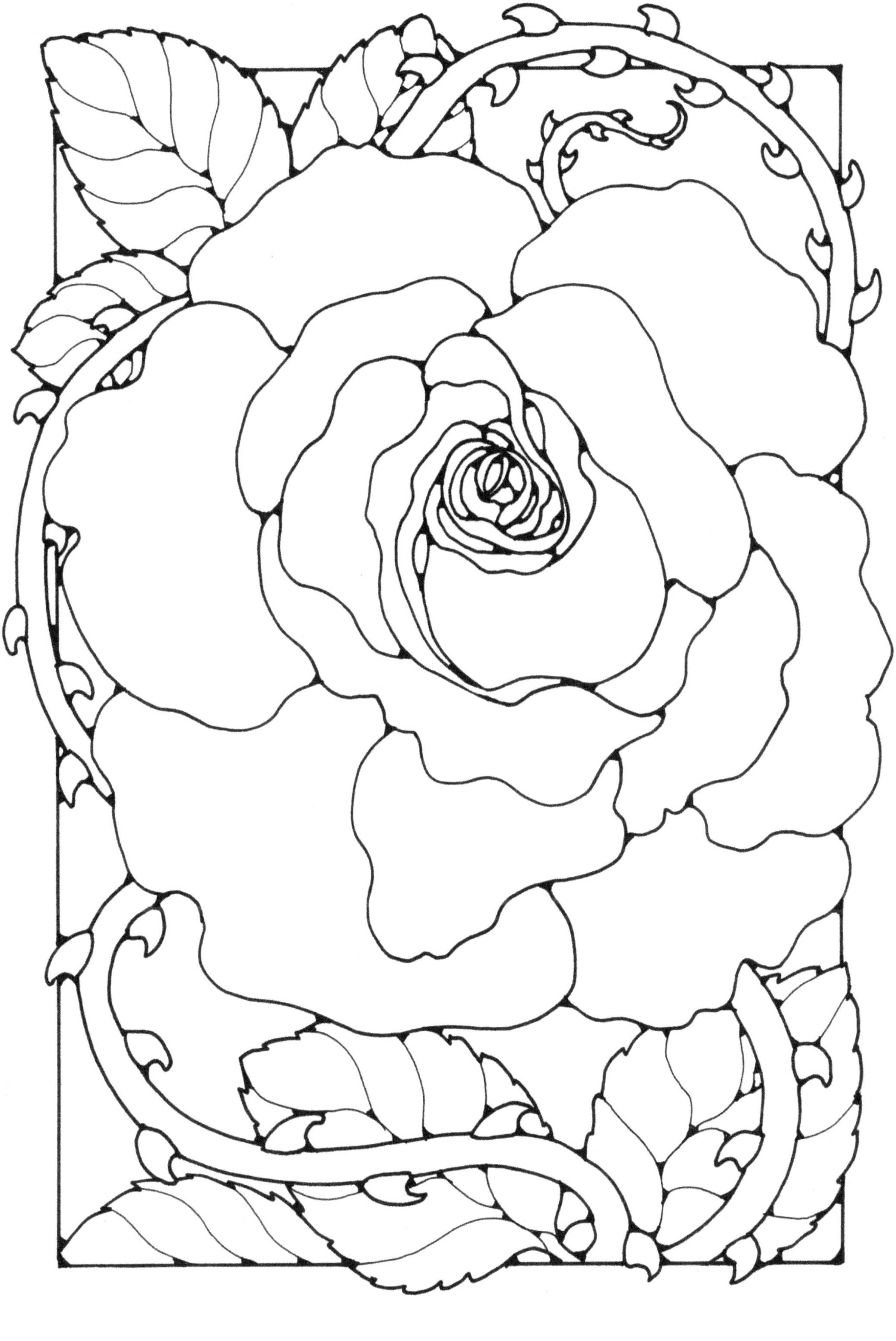

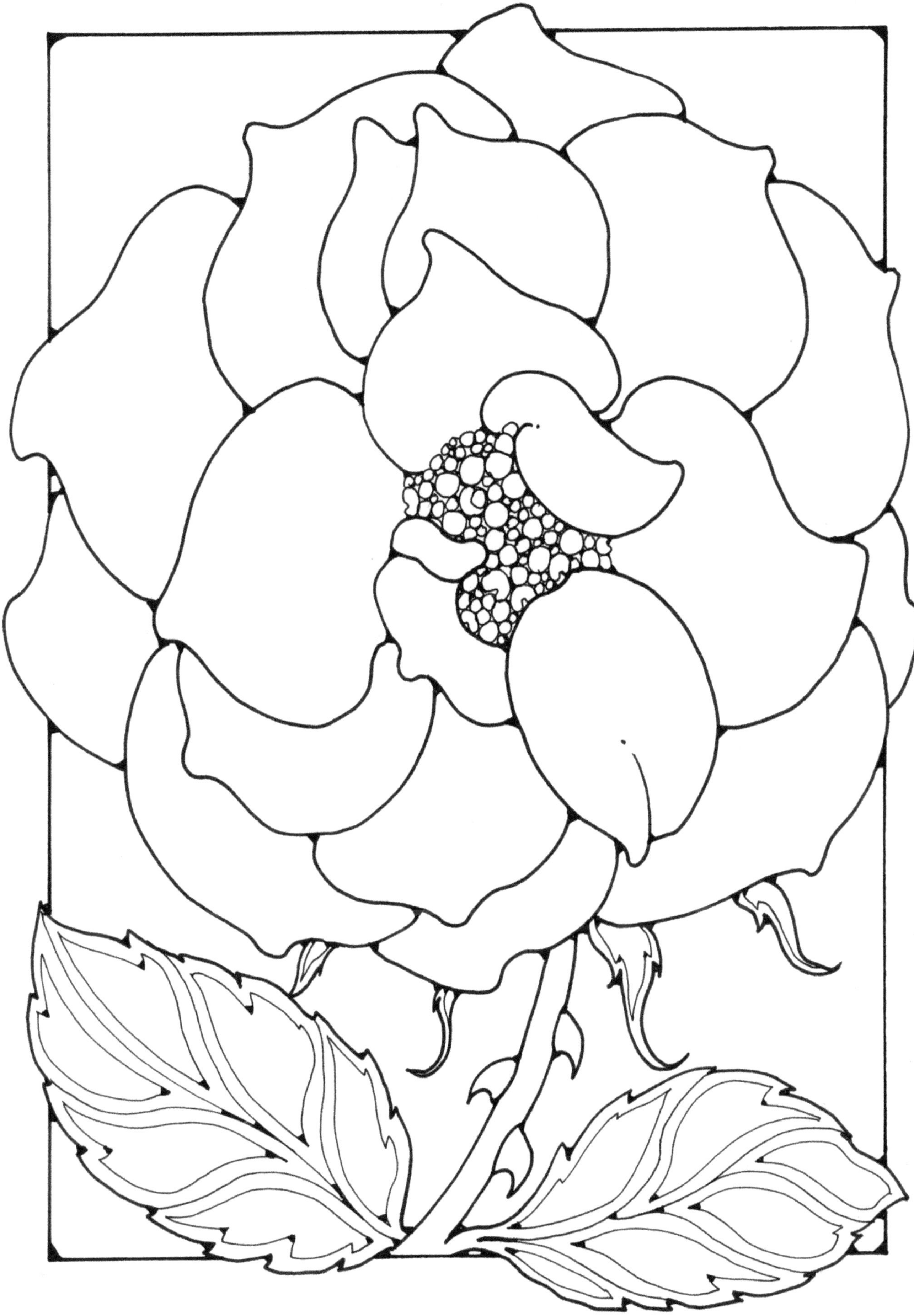

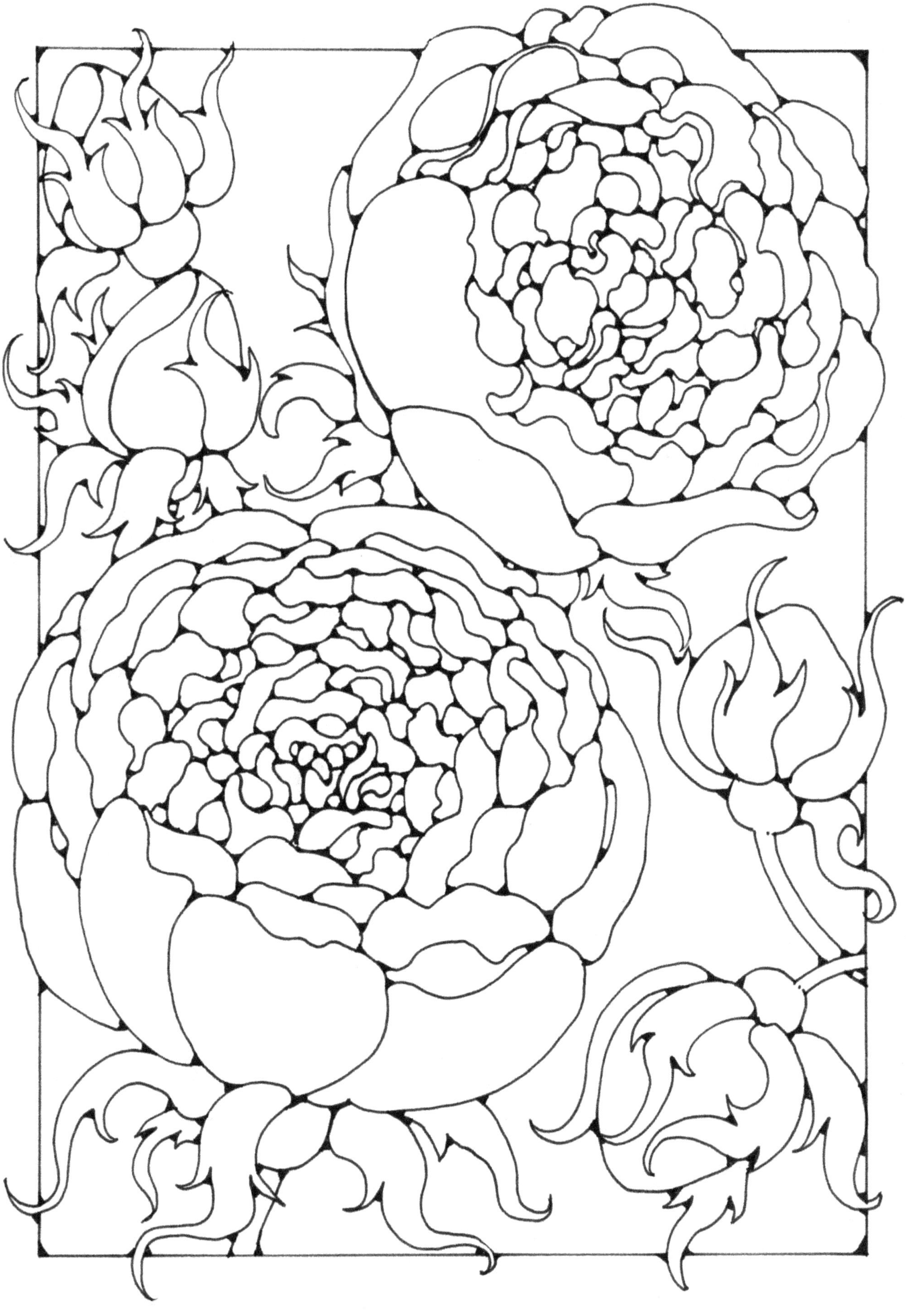

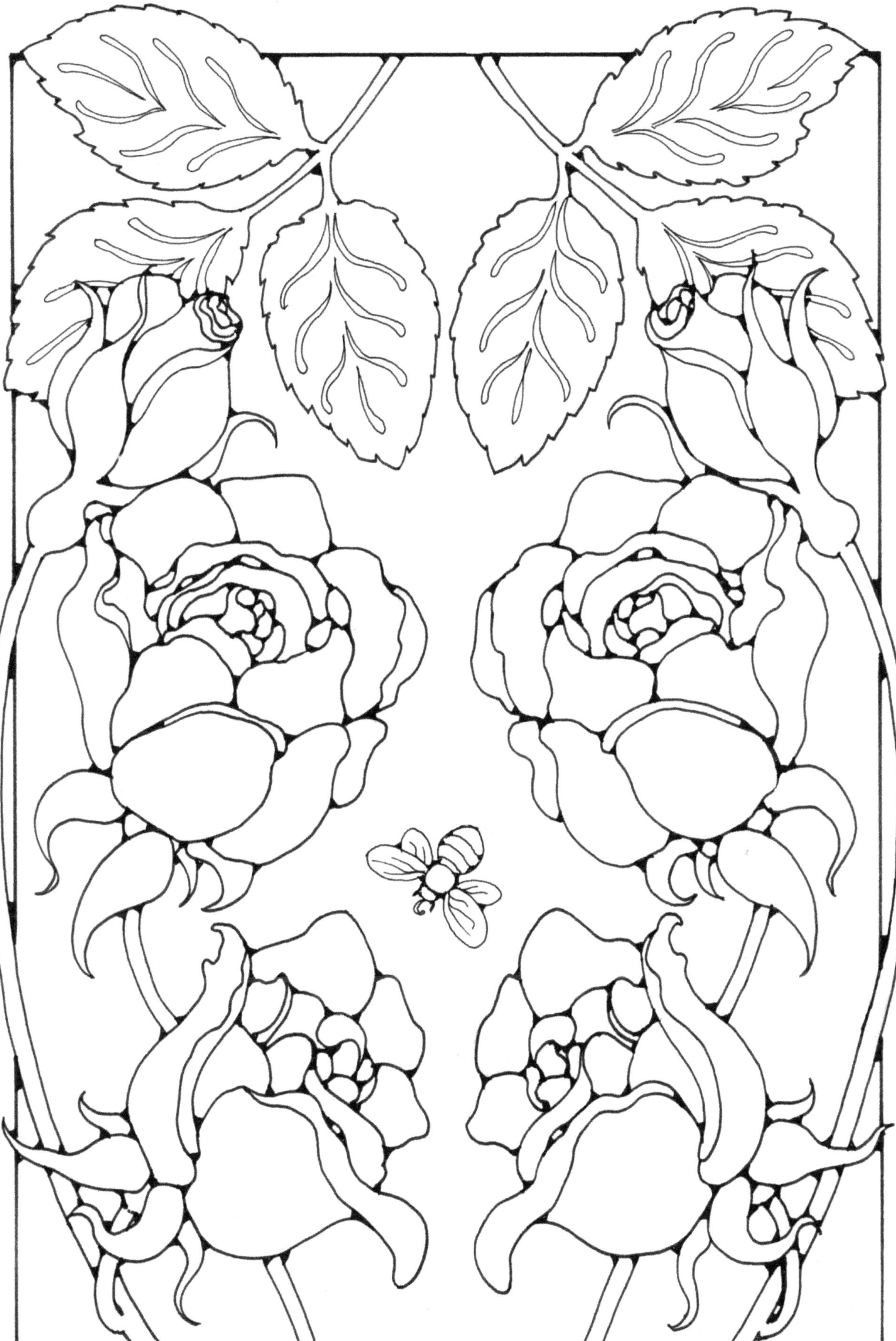

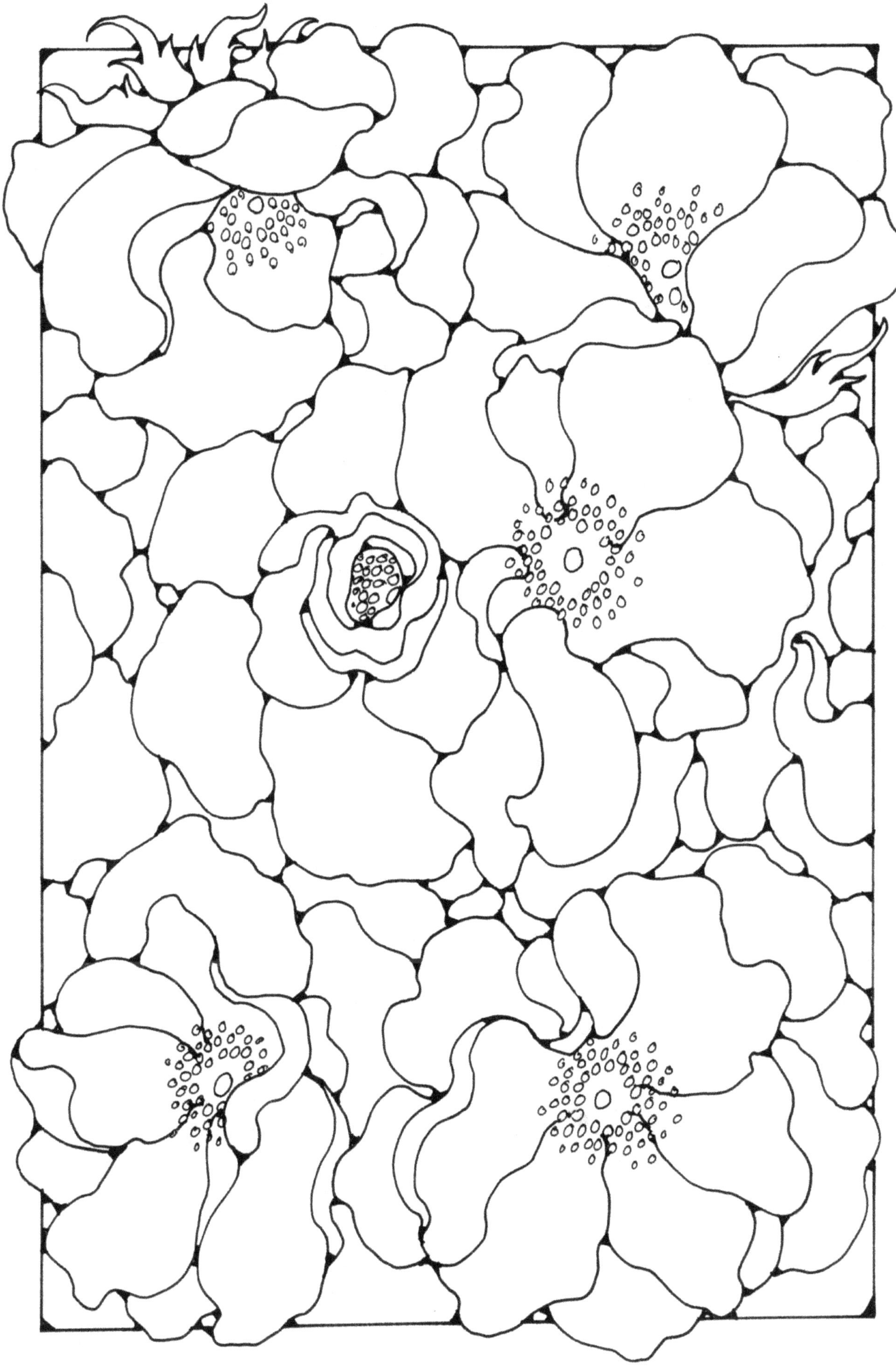

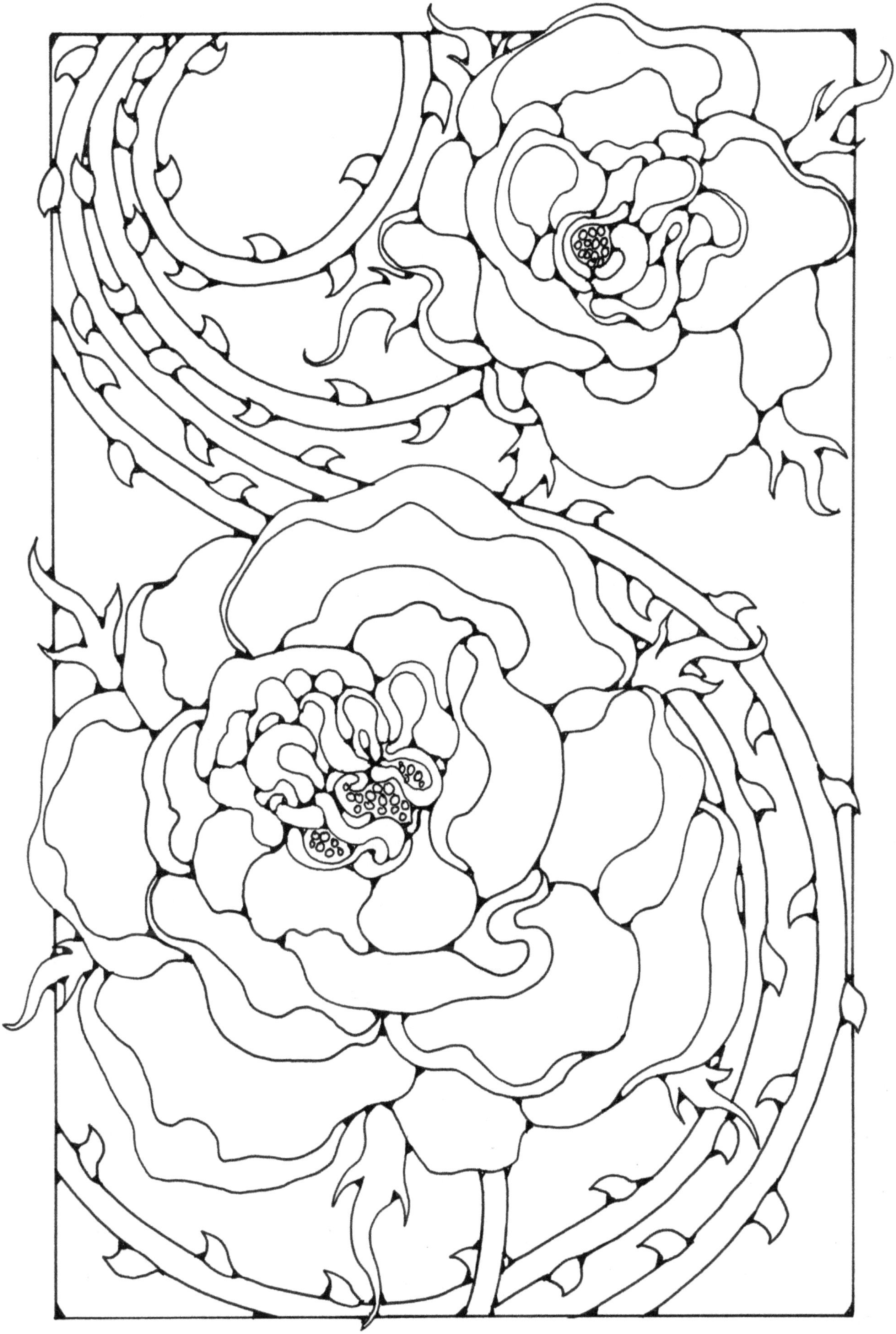

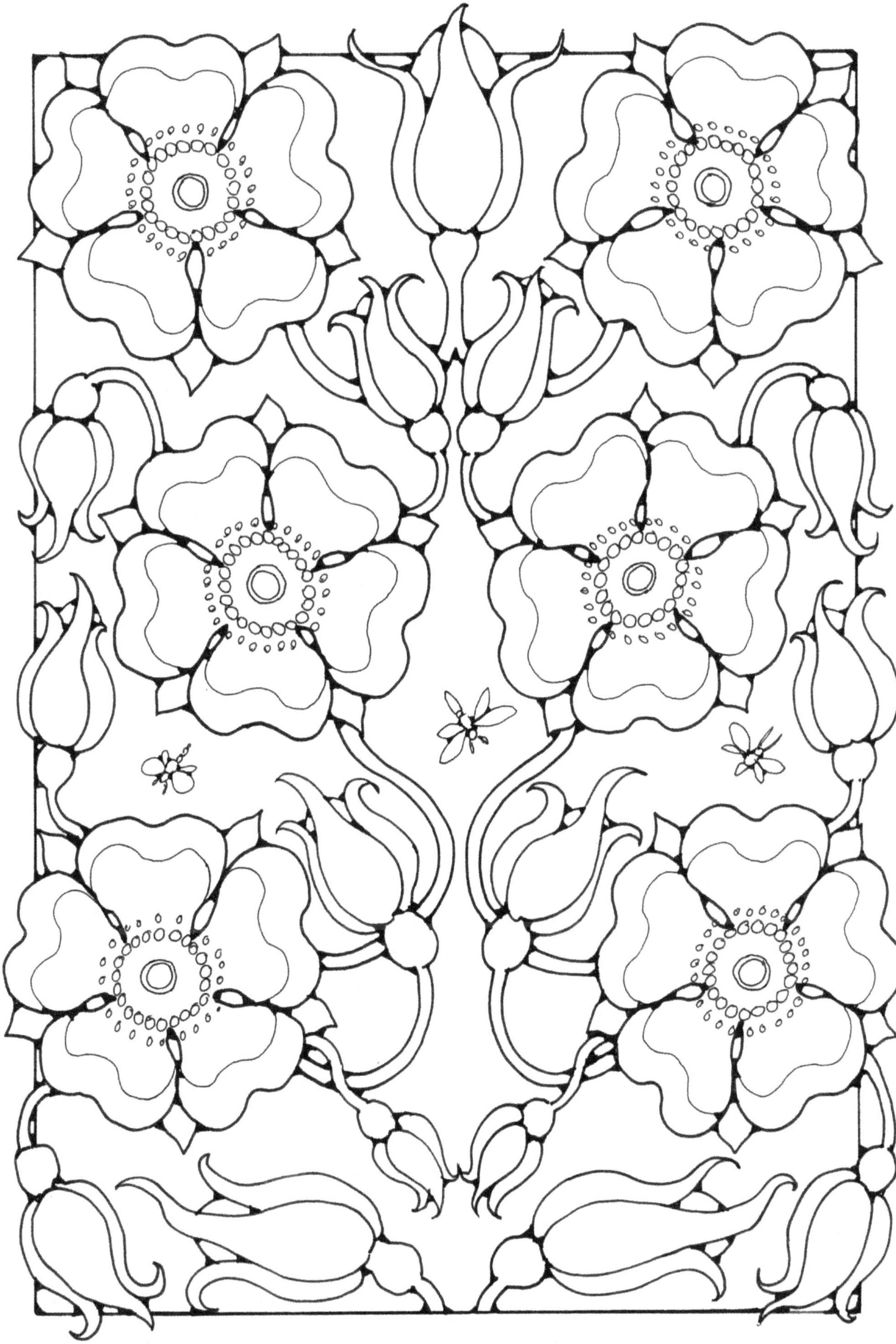

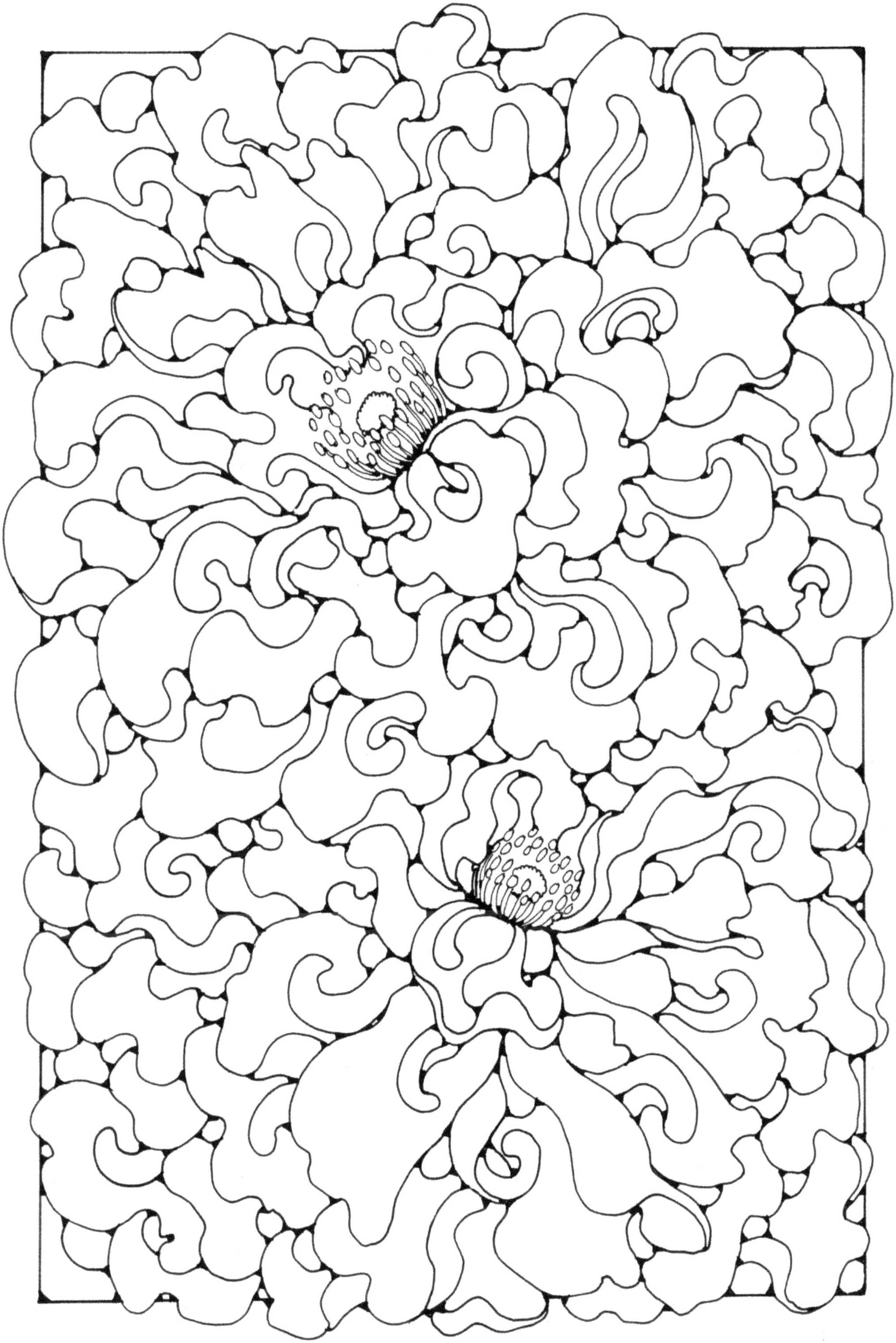

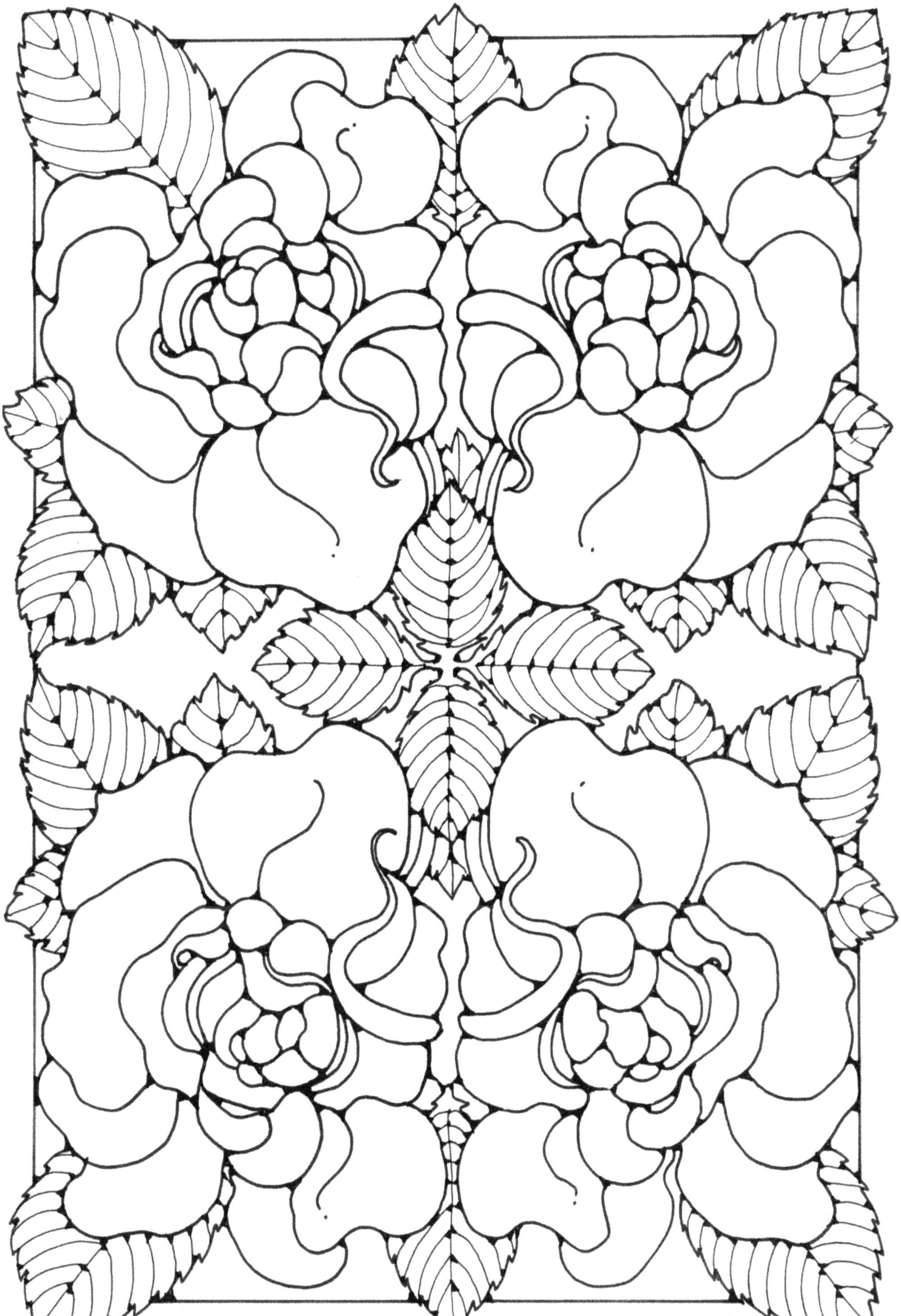

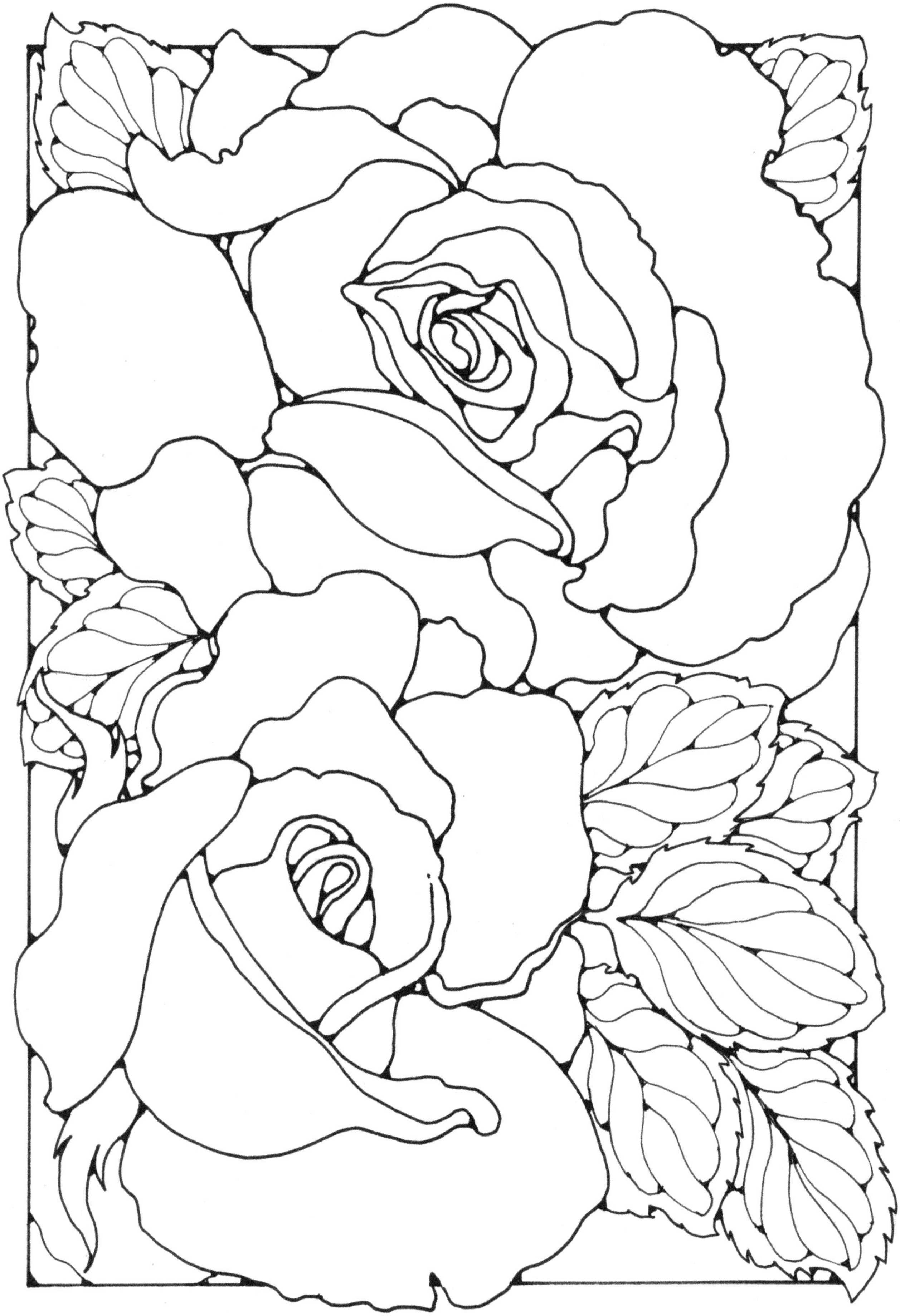

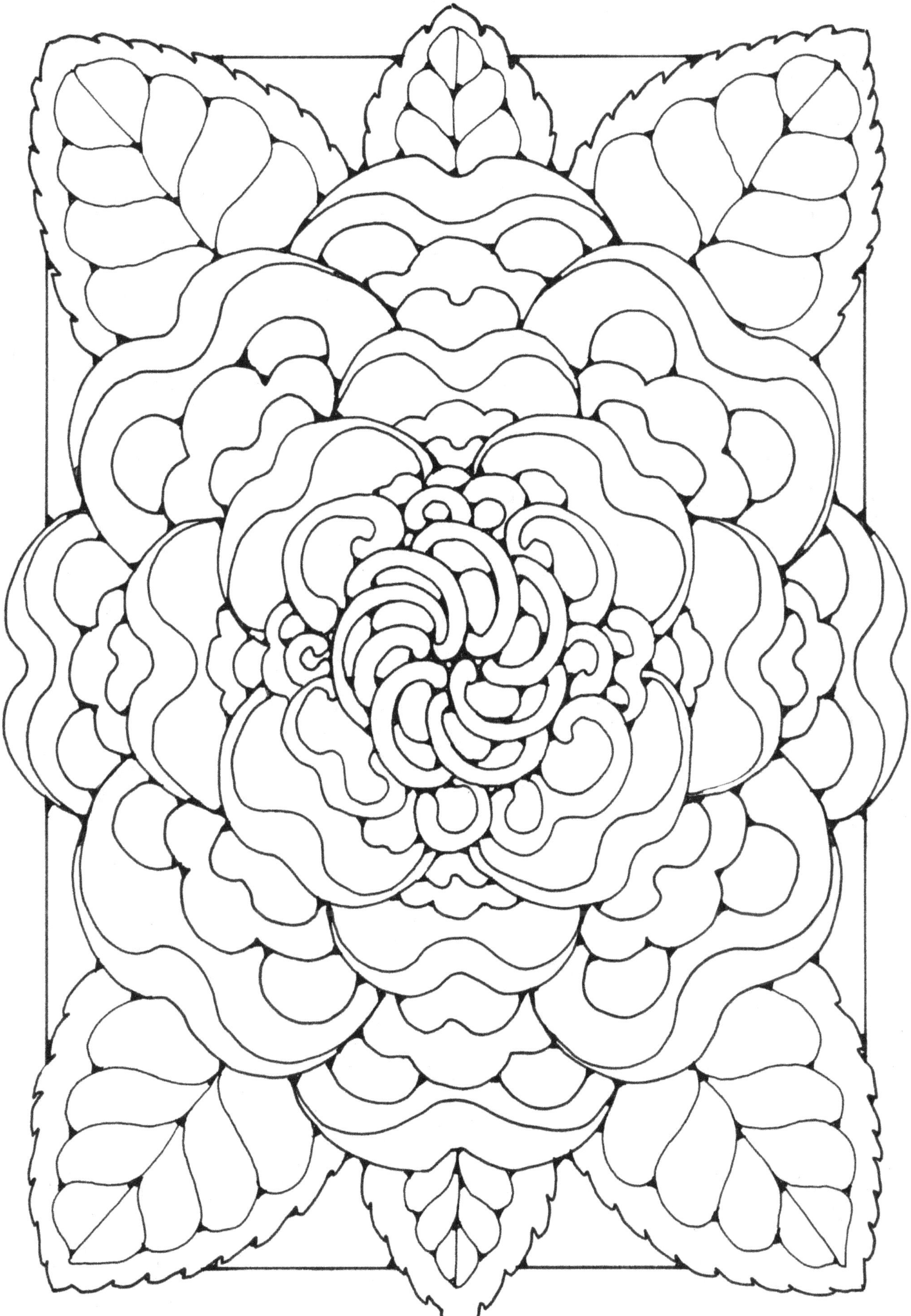

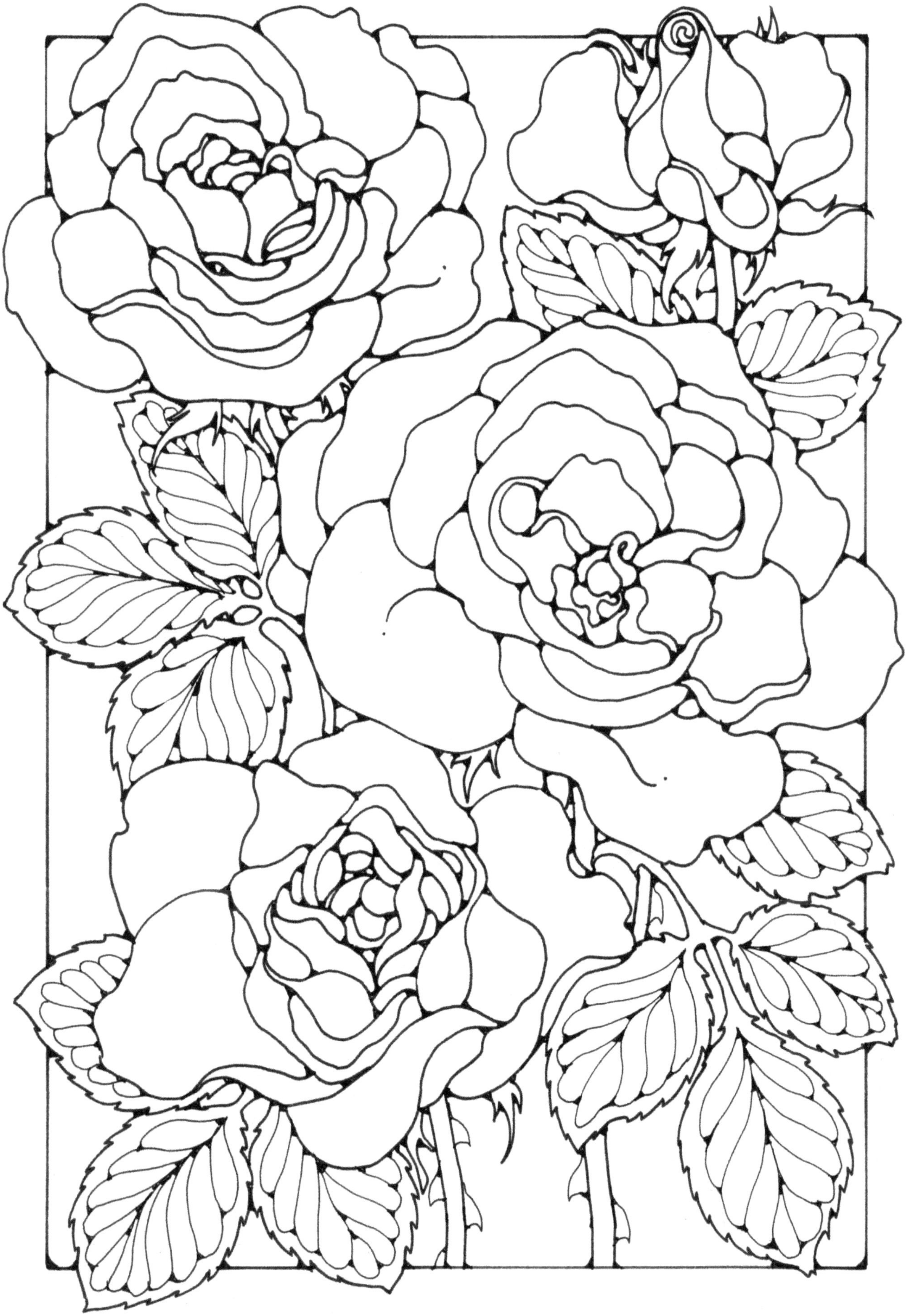

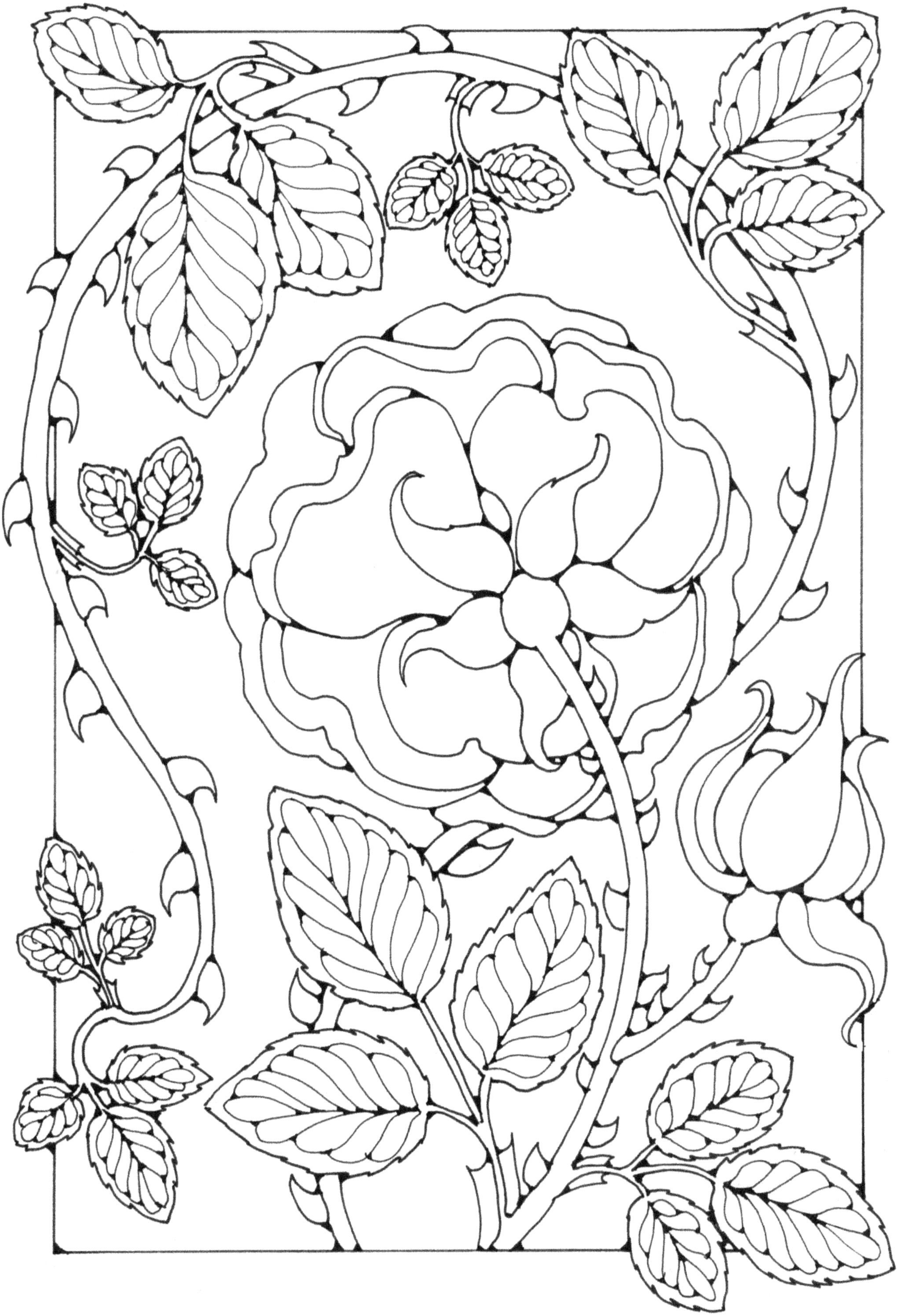

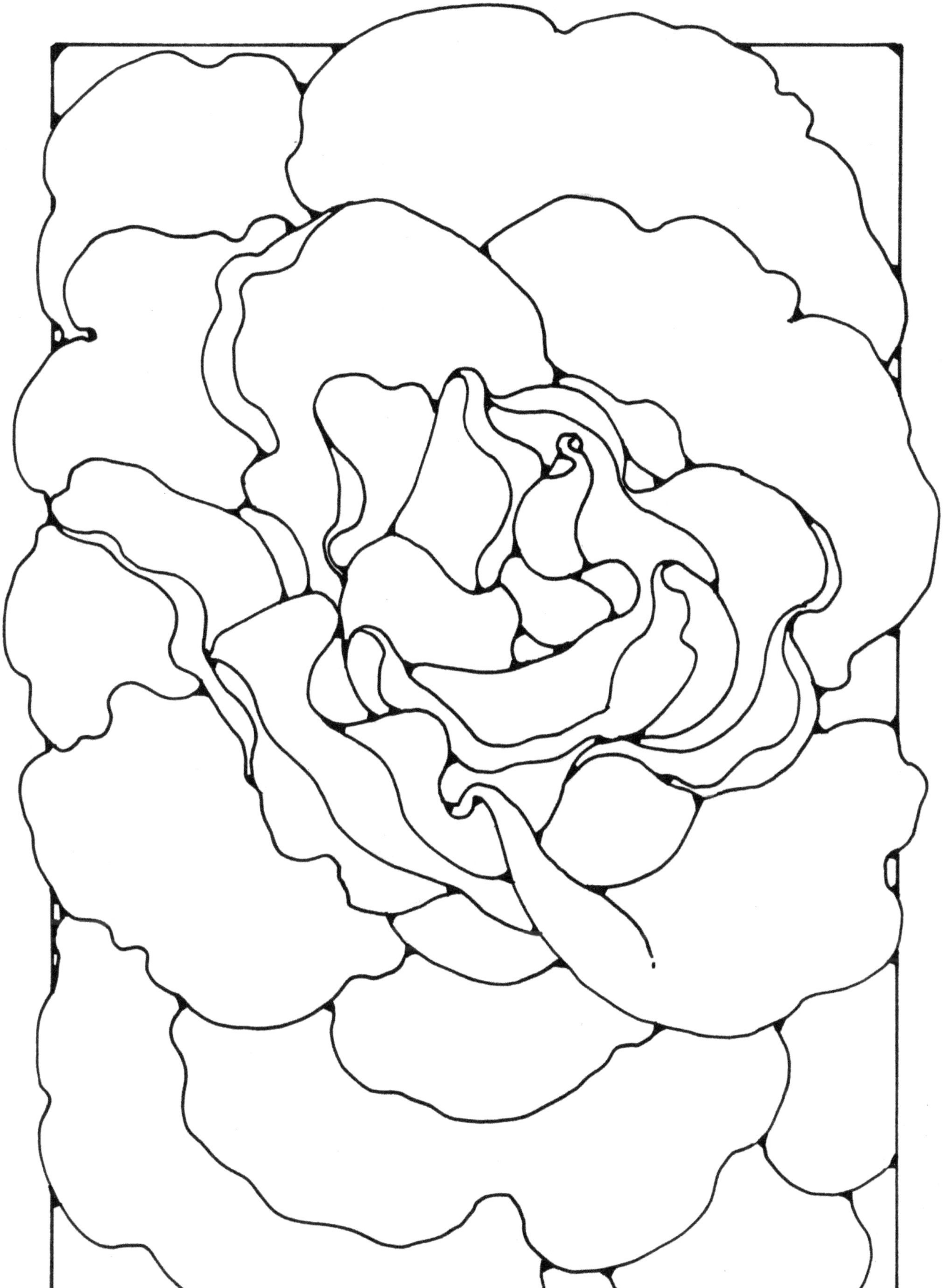

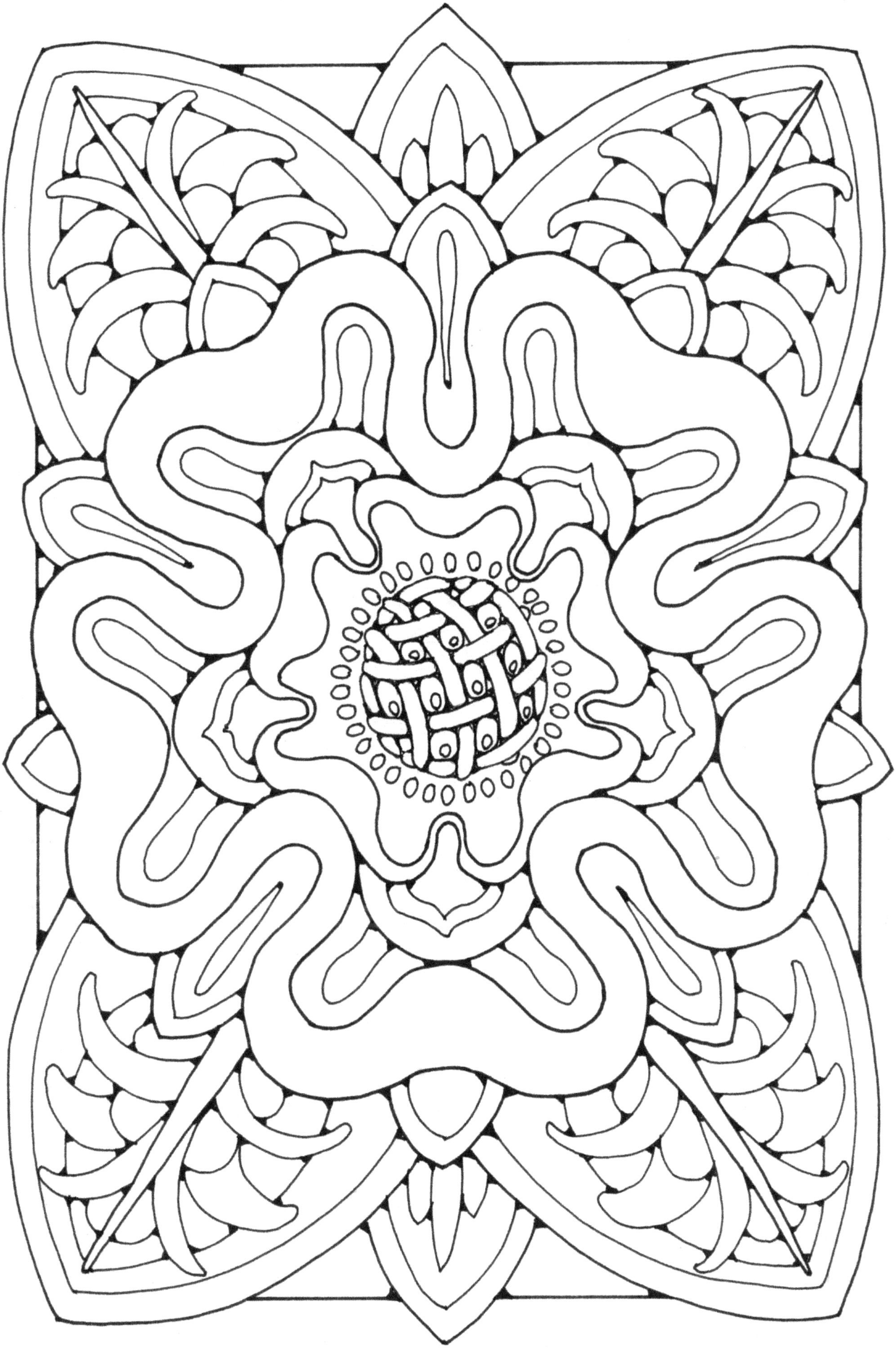

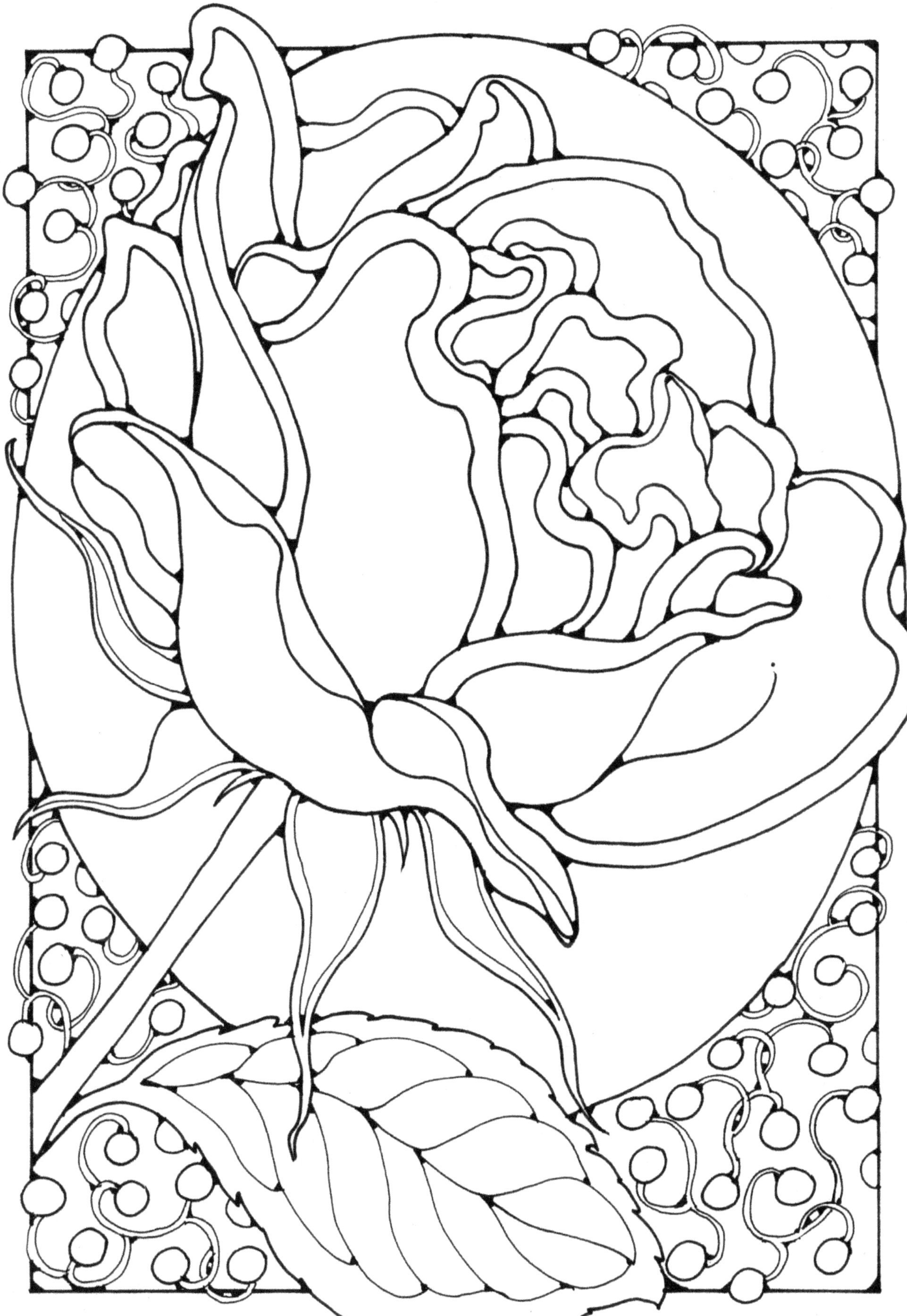

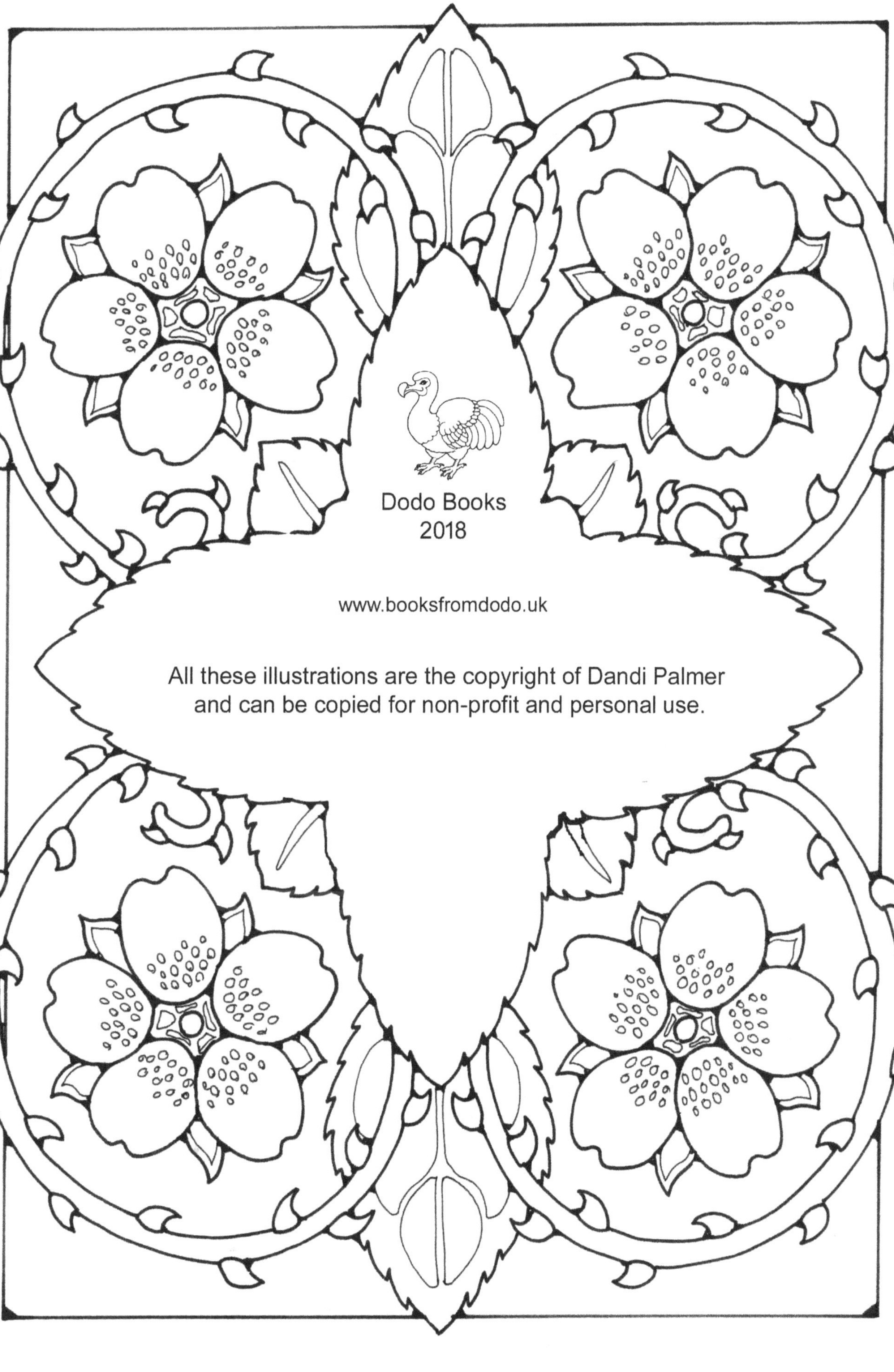

Dodo Books
2018

www.booksfromdodo.uk

www.ingramcontent.com/pod-product-compliance
Lightning Source LLC
Chambersburg PA
CBHW081220020426
42331CB00012B/3057